Flannery on Business Development, Marketing, and Sales for Lawyers

William J. Flannery, Jr.

A WJF INSTITUTE PUBLICATION

Published by William J. Flannery, Jr.
www.wjfinstitute.com

ISBN: 978-1463610456

Printed in the United States of America.

TABLE OF CONTENTS

ACKNOWLEDGMENTS

Special thanks to:

All of The WJF Institute Clients; who helped me write and helped edit these articles.

My Many Fellow Consultants; whose ideas I have used and whose generous advice made many of these articles significantly more interesting.

The Staff and Instructors of The WJF Institute; whose long hours and hard work make my life easier and more rewarding.

INTRODUCTION

Marketing has been a way of life for me since 1963. This collection of articles reflects my experience and thoughts as well as those who have influenced my career. Many of you are not marketing consultants and probably don't want to be, however, the message that these articles carry is the need for all of us to focus on:

> Our Clients,
> Their Needs, and
> How we can best serve them profitably.

Austin 2007

1

Seven Missing Links: The Sales Lessons That Law Firms Still Must Learn from the Corporate World

A WJF Institute White Paper

Clarence Sheftall, possibly the best law book salesman of our time, once articulated the Golden Rule of sales. He said, "I never bought anything from someone I didn't like, even if I needed it."

As good as this advice is, I wonder how many lawyers feel instead that clients don't need to like them; that results or the quality of the work product are what matters. The lawyers' view of business relationships and work product is somewhat misguided. It misses the point that, in a professional engagement, the trust placed in you by the client is an essential part of the results and how the client views the work product quality.

Rapport (liking) leads to trust and trust becomes the glue that binds the parties in a business relationship. Trust and liking the seller are two inseparable components that are necessary to make up a successful sale and a business relationship. Trust in this context means more than assuming that the seller won't pick your pocket. Trust is what will make the buyer's interest the seller's number one priority.

Profitable business relationships and sales have many things in common, not the least of which is this thing called trust. Indeed, trust is the foundation and prerequisite for any successful sale and, eventually, a profitable long-term relationship. To quote Buck Rogers, the renowned former VP of Sales for IBM, "Nothing happens in this world until somebody sells something to someone."

When we look at the current state-of-the-art in the legal profession, we discover that law firms have developed more powerful and sophisticated marketing engines than would have likely been imagined possible twenty-five years ago. A very few cutting-edge law firm marketing departments have achieved significant success fostering the kind of business development environment that supports a true "sales culture." Sales is basically finding a need and filling it. Helping clients with their needs is the major mission of all good lawyers.

But that next step has been very slow to happen. Despite the notable efforts of some firms to recruit "sales managers," the transition to a true sales culture still mystifies many law firms. There is a reason why – actually seven reasons why. These are the missing links to sales – the strategies and tactics that the corporate world identified many decades ago and have become the guiding principles of our modern corporate sales cultures.

They are:

➢ Skills to Sell

➢ Institutionalized Sales Process

➢ Major Account Management

➢ New Prospect Marketing

> ➤ Product Marketing

> ➤ Compensation

> ➤ Measurements for Success

Let's take a closer look at these missing links and consider their specific relevance for law firms.

Skills to Sell. In the corporate world, these skills are given a very special premium. They are stand-alone assets that define a separate and highly valued professional sector. Some people have management skills, some people have technical skills, and some people have sales skills. If you've got all three, you can be Jack Welch; however, the sales force need not have any skills except sales skills to be highly valued and highly placed on the corporate hierarchy. Without an effective sales force, the products and services never leave the plant, the office or other facilities. And, to be effective, everyone on that sales force shares a common vocabulary and culture.

Lawyers instinctively recoil from sales culture and jargon. Many lawyers view salespeople as less intelligent. Lawyers feel that salespeople are superficial, especially compared to professionals like themselves with substantive (i.e., technical) knowledge of patent law, corporate finance or the rules of evidence.

Here is the first and biggest difference between marketing and sales at law firms. Marketing can be technical in the sense that a substantive newsletter about patent law accomplishes a marketing purpose. So lawyers can sign off on marketing, but stop short at sales. However it is important for lawyers to understand that marketing does not build interpersonal business relationships. It is "good selling" that creates trust, trustworthiness and "liking".

To erase this synapse between marketing and selling, we

3

must teach lawyers that high-energy sales cultures, with their own language and values, are what distinguishes successful sales organizations from the less successful. The corporate world uses skills training to create and develop a successful sales force. All corporate sales executives start their careers in a structured sales training program ranging from one week to one year.

Typically, these highly sophisticated training programs are held in a campus learning environment. The curriculum includes structuring the sales call, analyzing customer needs, understanding and predicting buyer behavior, developing communications and presentations skills, writing proposals, product demonstrations, briefing customers on critical services, and building customer loyalty. The better programs use case studies, videotaping of sales executives and work presentations, in addition to on-site visits with experienced and successful salespeople who relate their success stories.

The objective of these sales training "universities" is to send a skilled group of sales executives into the field. Even the most experienced sales trainers that we have hired at The WJF Institute are required to go through an entire training course. The purpose is precisely to ensure what so many lawyers revile: a common sales culture.

The IBM or Intel sales force needs to go about its day-to-day activities the "IBM way" or the "Intel way." Large sales organizations cannot afford to have people "off the ranch;" i.e., doing things in their own idiosyncratic way. Graduates are sent back to their respective offices equipped to compete, or they are washed out if they fail to meet the skills standards set by the company's sales managers.

Unsophisticated law firms have failed to consider sales training as a prerequisite to a partner's professional development. Many firms have taken the approach that it is either in a partner's DNA to be a rainmaker or it's not. Those rainmakers then become targets and romanced by other law firms seeking to grow by hiring laterals. Or, as permanent fixtures at their firms, they rule the roost, often with no sales or management skills to

4

justify their institutional power. The other lawyers that are "non-naturals" or drought makers are banished to the production center, which wastes, not only human resource, but potentially significant and unanticipated revenue sources for the firm.

Along with their fearful thrall to the sales "natural," lawyers entertain an opposing, but equally spurious notion that clients make selections based on the perceived intellect of the lawyer-seller. It's a notion that further demeans their idea of sales skills as the client selection process is presumed to be scientific and rigid without regard to the skills of the lawyer-seller.

In fact, buying patterns and market conditions have never supported the scientific selection model. That model is flawed because, as Mr. Sheftall would agree, it has nothing to do with creating, developing, enhancing, growing relationships and trust building. So we have the worst of two false propositions at most law firms. Either only preternaturally gifted rainmaker lawyers can sell. Or, selling does not matter in any event.

If firms do identify sales skills as a need, they often use rainmakers to train and mentor, in those instances when the rainmaker is willing to share the glory. In our experience, this training is doomed to failure due to a lack of understanding of what these rainmakers actually do to be successful. The "mentoring" and training tends to be unstructured, personality-based or other irrelevant criteria.

Research shows that the effect of mentoring can be negative if the mentors are few in number and their protégés cannot adapt the mentor's business development or presentation styles. Based on our 16 years working with law firms and 32 years of business experience, we are convinced that a structured, formal sales skills training program, developed from the ground up is the best solution. The cost of doing it right is small compared to the cost of doing it wrong continuously. The greatest risks are that business development will be banished to the "back burner" and the mentors will suffer the loss of credibility when nothing happens.

Institutionalized Sales Process. Successful global sales organizations use a clear sales process to manage their sales efforts. Without such a sales process in place, sales representatives in New York could be making recommendations to their New York customers that directly contradict with what their Hong Kong counterparts are recommending to their Hong Kong customers. Without a sales process that is followed by all, the chances of a sales rep making a pitch at the wrong time is likely. A worldwide sales process is thus especially critical with sophisticated global customers. Lastly and most importantly, a sales process is critical in moving from simple rapport with the customer to that of a trusted advisor.

Sales teams hold formal and comprehensive account management meetings annually in January to develop the sales plans for a specific account. In addition to a sales process for the account, and an overall strategy, the sales force will need a clear understandable process for each sales call. If your sales force is multi-lingual, the process needs to be simple, concise, and accessible. (It should not be complex under any circumstances.)

Typically, the sales call process has no more than six stages and usually just four: Plan the call. Identify what the customer needs. Present your capability for meeting the need. Ask the customer to define the process for moving forward to a favorable decision.

It is a process eminently adaptable for both products and services. It works for both new prospects and current customers as well. Customer Relationship Management software is an invaluable and perhaps necessary tool as it allows the sales force and individual sales representatives to identify where they are with each client/prospect and the next steps in the process.

An institutionalized process, with Customer Relationship Management software to support it, is crucial with small accounts. From a management standpoint, small accounts are often numerous and potentially unwieldy without formalized procedures. This market segment may lend itself to groupings.

Industry-focused, geographic-focused or product-focused teams are often the solution to creating an opportunity to gain market share.

Major Account Management. It is a generally accepted premise in sales that most new business comes from existing customers. As part of the institutionalized sales process discussed above, corporations have, (and law firms need) formalized sales teams. Complementing these are account management teams for major customers that function by creatively dovetailing customer service with the development of new business opportunities that result from superior customer service. These teams are made up of marketers, salespeople and administrative types.

The leaders of these teams have many titles. The most widely used is Global Account Manager (GAM). The equivalent in a law firm might be called a Client Relationship Manager (CRM). The CRM is the team linchpin. Especially in the flat environment of a law firm, the CRM does not own the client but he or she must be someone the client will trust and, indeed, like. For these CRMs, the theme returns emphatically to the advice from Clarence Sheftall that began this discussion. Sales is all about trust, and the CRM should have as their mission to engender trust. The CRM's greatest asset is their ability to build trust.

The CRM's time to manage the account should be non-billable. Corporations have developed immense new revenues because the GAM's time is used effectively overseeing key relationships. In a law firm, it can be difficult indeed to persuade partners to look beyond billable hours. Yet the ones that can do so will institutionalize the sales process – and, by definition, that will amply reward the short-term utilization sacrifice. A CRM who cannot increase profitability with existing clients is the wrong CRM.

At the same time, the CRM should be practicing law to maintain his or her credibility with both the lawyer team and the client. Their role provides an in-the-trenches perspective on how and where legal services to the client can improve or expand. The legal work is billable; the team management time is not. Make it clear to the client that the service oversight is not a cost add-on.

The CRM grows the account by assisting the client in the preparation of annual legal budget projections. To achieve these projections, the CRM must understand the client's business well enough to forecast services across the whole spectrum of client needs. From a sales perspective, the CRM is thus directly engaged – simply by virtue of his or her role as forecaster – in two of the WJF Institute's four sales stages: identifying client needs and presenting the firm's capacity to meet them.

For an expanded discussion of these client relationship teams, and how they can operate in the context of a law firm, see our article, It's The Client, Stupid: How to Avoid Marketing Malpractice with Large Key Clients, at www.wjfinstitute.com.

New Prospect Marketing. We have examined the marketing/sales synapse, observing how sophisticated law firms have become in their marketing efforts and their lack of sophistication in their sales efforts. But just as client service in the form of CRM dovetails with sales, so too is there an element of marketing that is inextricably bound up with the sales sensibility and with sales technique.

When corporations go after new market segments – when they're targeting new demographic segments, or when they are introducing new products or services to established consumer blocs – they research those segments. The corporate marketing departments look to uncover customer buying patterns. They define ongoing needs. Maybe a retail chain sets up an on-premise ATM because they've done enough homework to know that the people who buy their goods will welcome the easy availability of cash. Casinos are clearly way ahead of the learning curve with this kind of research.

As we cannot repeat too often, defining the needs of the

buyer is part of the sales process. Those definitions must emerge as a result of combined marketing and sales efforts. Corporations, though, go further in combining marketing and sales activity. Many companies now have their top sales people do the marketing themselves, or at least participate intimately with the marketing departments. The salespeople themselves uncover who the new prospects are and, because they are part of the marketing process (i.e., prospect identification process), there is no need for a handoff from marketing to sales. The salespeople can segue at once to the sales phase, often by cold-calling the prospects that have been identified, or by turning up at the business shows where these or similar prospects are likely to be found.

Often, too, salespeople directly participate in marketing because the strategy at hand is to achieve further and better industry penetration. "Better" penetration in the sense that the goal is to upgrade the customer lists within the particular industry, from lower- to higher-profit margin potential.

For law firms, such new prospect marketing, with the implicit dovetailing of marketing and sales, is a daunting but exciting prospect. Those few firms that have brought on sales managers are taking positive steps in this direction. These sales managers need to have direct contact with clients to be successful.

Law firm new client efforts or prospecting is, for the most part, serendipitous and unorganized. Targeting the most profitable clients and work must be segmented, just as current client efforts are profitably segmented. The top-of-the-list targets should be those businesses and organizations that the firms can move up the industry ladder to the best-of-breed clients. Reputation in the industry plays a big part; however, contact needs to be made with the decision makers in these new prospects. Referrals from current clients are the easiest path but often clients are reluctant to go public with their law firm affiliations, especially with competitors.

The bottom line may be a cold call on the CEO or General Counsel as the only way to get access. Cold calling has its own

9

set of challenges. Lawyers don't like to get cold calls and see them as unprofessional. Cold calls from stockbrokers or financial planners are different than cold calls on businesses. Unlike broker cold calls, the focus of the lawyers' efforts are to help companies and their executives achieve business goals, not personal investment strategies. We have seen that cold calling efforts in accounting, consulting and sales organizations actually have a high degree of success. The following are part of the successful implementation:

> Effective targeting. Research on the prospective client's needs is critical.

> Building the story. Using the research, the caller should earn the buyer's interest within the first several minutes of the call.

> Always seek a face-to-face meeting.

> Have a clear process to move the non-buyer to a buyer.

> Earn the trust of the potential client by focusing on their unmet needs if possible. Unmet needs are the seller's greatest opportunity.

> If you fail to get the business on the first visit, leave the door open for follow-up face-to-face visits.

> Persistence and empathy with the potential buyer are two qualities that have high payoff.

The new sales manager or business development manager can be of great value to the firm if they manage this process rather than leave it to individual lawyers to follow-up.

Another real payoff for most law firms is the closer working relationship that develops between their marketing departments and their top rainmakers, and the willingness of those rainmakers to be more directly involved in market research and marketing plan development, just as their counterparts among the top salespeople at corporations have crossed the line and taken on marketing roles as well.

Product Marketing. Here we have a strategic complement to sales. Product marketing's mission as a corporate department is to better identify what you are selling and what you should be selling. The opportunity to gain greater market share comes when the customer's latent needs can be identified and met. This is a form of niche marketing applicable to both products and services. As Proctor Houston, my first IBM Branch Manager, used to say, "Find a need and fill it."

It is often forgotten that niche marketing applies as much to what is being sold as who is being sold. In the technology business, it's calling "marketing the box," with that "box" being a particular product niche: servers, PCs, or whatever. Product marketing further complements new prospect marketing because, by exploiting the sales potential of your newest and best product, you can more effectively target the new prospects and penetrate their industries.

For law firms, and for other professional service organizations, simply replace "newest and best product" with "core competence." You achieve client growth, and entrée to their industries, by leading with your best. It is an exceptionally important point, and not nearly as obvious as it sounds. Consider how many law firms try to penetrate, for example, the pharmaceutical industry by leading with their competent but undistinguished (and indistinguishable) employment practitioners or with their equally undifferentiated tax lawyers. The thinking is we'll sneak in with those lawyers, who will then be able to forge relationships with the client that will create space for our truly distinguished FDA regulatory experts to march into later, like triumphant centurions.

It only happens that way, to the best of my knowledge, in rare circumstances and frequently by chance. I would venture to say that to build your sales efforts in the corporate world using that approach would be financial suicide.

Compensation. Money drives sales, and corporations use it to encourage more sales. If they did not, they would go out of business. But where some corporations, and many law firms, err in their sales reward programs is by being unselective, by being wholly driven by volume, and by letting volume define the criteria for success.

Success goes beyond these surface returns. Let us say that sales rep Smith brings home $1 million in new sales in an industry where you are competing with 1,000 other companies, 500 of which are 50 times your size. That $1 million is going to stay flat. You do not have market share. You never will.

Meanwhile, sales rep Jones brings home $500,000 in new sales in a growth industry where you are competing with 10 other companies, none of which is as big as you. You have market share. And, because you have market share, you will grow with that industry. Depending on the industry, the near- and long-term returns could be incalculable.

So, are you going to reward sales rep Jones 50 percent less than sales rep Smith?

Similarly, the right approach to compensation recognizes profits, not just revenue. Let's say there is a 3% margin on sales rep Smith's $1 million in sales. But there is a 70% margin on sales rep Jones's $500,000 in sales. Again, are you going to reward sales rep Jones 50% less than sales rep Smith?

In fact, that's what law firms do every day. What commands power at a law firm? Books of business. What defines those books? Revenue. Revenue and nothing else. The revenue may derive from a dying client industry. No matter. The revenue may demand exorbitant overhead to maintain. No matter.

"Eat-what-you-kill" cultures particularly suffer from their oversimplified compensation formulas, exacerbated because "origination" as a criterion for compensation puts no particular value on one form of business versus another. The rules of compensation may not be practiced well by all corporations, but corporate cultures are still leagues beyond law firms and most other professional organizations.

There are ten rules of compensation law firm managers should memorize.

1. It must be fairly applied. For law firms, fairness often means rewarding a collective sales effort, not just crediting the so-called "originator" of the client contact.

2. It needs to be clearly understood. The backstage intrigues of executive committees and compensation committees often undermine honest disclosure of how the compensation system actually works in practice.

3. It should produce a desired behavior or strategy. That behavior should always include cooperativeness and teamwork, not just initiative and aggressiveness.

4. It must be flexible enough to allow for exceptions. Perhaps a deal falls through at the last moment because of an unforeseeable crisis or tragedy affecting the buyer. Rewarding the sales rep anyway is not only fair, it is smart.

5. It must be clearly measurable. You can deviate from the numbers if there is a good reason to, and if you can articulate that reason, but the numbers have to be there as the coherent starting point.

6. It should drive profit, not hours. Hours, of course, equate with sales revenue in the example of Messrs. Smith and Jones above.

7. It should be adjusted frequently to be responsive to the

market. Market changes include both changes on the demand side, and changes in the growth and scope of your competition.

8. It should be used as an incentive by the partners. Partners may, in some cultures, want to extend sales incentives to their associates. (At many law firms, hell will freeze over first.)

9. It should include recognition, not just monetary rewards. Recognition is especially necessary if, in our example above, sales rep Jones' higher-margin, lower-revenue sale does not gain him the institutional profile that sales rep Smith may gain with his high-revenue sale. Recognize sales rep Jones with some conspicuous institutional entitlement.

10. It should send a message to your clients. Rewarding sales based on quality rather than quantity means rewarding higher-quality work. Clients prefer Tiffany to K-Mart. They like to see lawyers rewarded for realization rather than utilization.

Measurements for Success. Corporations, to a far greater extent than most law and other professional firms, take the process full-circle. They measure the effects of their marketing and sales activity and they let the measurement criteria shape and define the next cycle of marketing and sales activity. In other words, they learn from experience and change what needs to be changed.

There are at least four fundamental measures of success. To an extent, they are all implicit in the marketing and sales dynamics we have discussed so far:

➤ Market share. As we've seen, it is a profound index of success. In a mature industry, it means you are a dominant "safety buy." In a growth industry, it could mean potentially unlimited future growth if the industry grows.

➤ Profitability index. Take a look at the profit margins on

last year's new business. Now take a look at the profit margins on this year's new business. The differential will tell the tale. If you're selling more and making less, you need to redefine your sales strategy.

➤ Account penetration. Client relations is a sales performance index, not just a quality-of-service index. How many more services are you providing to you core accounts on December 31 of this year than you were on December 31 of last year? Static relationships are vulnerable as clients are more likely to jettison a supplier on whom they are dependent for one service (irrespective of dollar volume or work volume) than for ten services.

➤ Year-end profitability. This, of course, is the highest tribunal. Remember, law firms as businesses are more revenue- and profit-driven than cost-sensitive. Unless a bad leasehold or retirement plan problem has eroded the bottom line, think income first and outgo second. Marketing and sales should be the highest-priority assessments as you read the year-end return and make plans to improve it.

****

We have, to be sure, indulged in some healthy generalizations in this discussion. Not all corporations offer exemplary sales cultures. Not all law firms are clueless. As we have noted, the progress law firms have made in marketing would not have been anticipated by the profession's marketing pioneers in the 1980s and early 1990s.

There is mind set in the corporate world that law firms do not have. The corporate world sees their sales force as heroes. In most law firms, sales is considered to be as close to a four letter word as one could imagine. It seems to me that law firms should view business development or "sales" as part of being a good lawyer. Great business developers see their client relationships in terms of mutual trust, not exploitation. When a client makes a buying decision, it is because of the trusted advice from outside counsel, not because of some "pitch" they were given by a "silver-tongued devil."

This article is the "tip of the iceberg." The skills, tactics, infrastructures and strategies that law firms will need are still under water. I see the competitive heat from clients and prospective clients in the marketplace as the catalyst to melting the iceberg and exposing the opportunity.

2

How To Make Client-Focused Business Development Teams Happen...With A Little Help From Henry Fonda

"Client-Focused Teams require additional leadership material that can only be drawn from the rank and file of the partnership."

They're as essential to the success of a law firm as an Executive Committee. Client-Focused Business Development Teams, hereafter referred to as **Client-Focused Teams**, represent the ideal approach to business development for law firms because they are predicated on teamwork – although teamwork is the one cultural essential all too often lacking in that land of lone wolves.

Client-Focused Teams are exactly what they sound like. A team of lawyers is formed, linked by common expertise, common industry knowledge, common interest and most importantly, a common client. The team identifies how to service the client, plans how to approach the client, pitch the client, and follows up afterward. It is a collective approach from beginning to end.

17

It works better than any other approach for at least two fundamental reasons. First, the very existence of a **Client-Focused Team** gives clients what they want but seldom get: an in-depth glimpse, not just of the sales skills of one premier rainmaker, but of the range of talent and expertise that will actually be assigned to their work if they do finally buy.

And second, the lawyers themselves learn by doing. Business development skills are disseminated throughout the firm. No longer are there just finders and minders (and never the twain shall meet). All team members are on their way to being rainmakers. Client consciousness and business development awareness permeate the institution to an ever greater degree.

For many law firms, it is still a long road from where they are today to the reality of **Client-Focused Teams**. Adding to the problem is that all firms do actually have client teams already in place, but the communication levels within teams (not to mention cross-communication and cross-selling among the different teams) are woefully deficient. Business development efforts become veritable shadow acts with occasionally motivated lawyers more or less conspiring behind the scenes to commit random acts of business development.

Were there no teams at all in place, our chore might be easier. We could create new models from the ground floor. Instead, we have to grapple with existing groups that resist or even oppose new initiatives to increase communication and redefine the responsibilities of each team member.

How do we cut through the dead wood and plant a few healthy **Client-Focused Team** seedlings?

The first and foremost issue is leadership. It's tough enough for most law firms to induce leadership at the firm-wide management level. **Client-Focused Teams** require additional leadership material that can only be drawn from the rank and file of the partnership.

Finding the right material for that leadership is the first step. In this article, we will introduce some modeling criteria that firms can use in meeting the challenge – including a few strikingly useful prototypes drawn from the American cinema.

But finding the right leaders is only the first step. Beyond that, these leaders need to be armed with a number of best practices designed to create, or recreate, **Client-Focused Teams**, and to manage team activities on a long-term basis.

Leadership: Style and Substance

It's not surprising that law firms suffer from a leadership dearth. Lawyers, after all, are essentially trained as artisans – highly intellectual artisans, but artisans nonetheless, with little of the organizational training that allows the corporate world to develop superior leaders within their ranks.

Like any other organization, a law firm can either select leaders or let those leaders evolve "organically;" in other words, self-select, either because they naturally assume responsibility or because their partners instinctively cede them that responsibility.

The organic approach is the most common one and, unfortunately, the least likely to be successful. Where there is no clear designated leader, a 10-30-60 rule applies. My observations, based on thirty years of working with law firms, has shown that effective leaders happily emerge only 10 percent of the time. 30% of the time, the team drifts or disbands altogether.

Worst of all, 60% of the time, the reins are seized by someone with no intrinsic leadership talent, but with a decidedly self-interested motive (money or power) for assuming command. In some instances, these non-leaders are positively dysfunctional individuals – not just lacking leadership qualities, but also by nature incapable of seeing beyond themselves.

Clearly, the firms that will thrive over the long haul are those that consciously and thoughtfully select and develop their leaders. For these firms, there are two bits of interrelated good news. First, you don't have to be a leader yourself in order to recognize one. Second, leadership is not ineffable: there are specific traits that can be spotted as qualifying one of your partners for the job, including:

> The Vision Thing. Leaders should be able to articulate some notion of what they want at the end of the day in terms of their own teams, their clients, and their firms. In business, "vision" can be summarized as a cogent answer to the burning question, "What Will Success Look Like?"

> Call to Action. Which one of your partners really gets things done? Chances are, he or she could not have gotten so much done without inspiring others to help.

> Focus. It's hard to get people to do things if you're so distracted they won't think it's really that important!

> Ethics. You can't lead people who don't trust you.

> Self-deployment. The old saw, "I wouldn't ask you to do anything I'm not willing to do" is a cardinal leadership principle.

> Opportunities for Others. Generosity inspires; so does the perception that a leader can actually help his team members in their careers.

> Motivates Others. You don't need locker room speeches. Instead, real leaders have an uncanny sense of what makes others want to act in a certain way.

> Provides Resources. Leaders inspire when they make it easier to succeed, not harder.

> Consensus builder. Valuing team members' input makes them feel like a part of the team.

> ➤ Trustworthy communicator. Leaders don't punish people for having opinions they don't agree with. Leaders who betray confidences won't lead for long.

> ➤ A great lawyer. It's not necessarily a matter of technical skills, but a wise client counselor or creative practitioner earns respect, especially in the legal profession.

> ➤ Team first, self second. Team members can always be inspired to serve the team when they sense that the leader has their best interest at heart.

You know these traits when you see them. Partners who exhibit all or most of these attributes should be groomed at once for leadership roles. The need is too great to waste the opportunity.

A Cinematic Exercise

Leadership selection naturally requires thoughtful deliberation among those making the selection. I would suggest a rather pleasant way to help guide these difficult deliberations: Sit down with your partners and watch a few movies!

Some years ago, The WJF Institute, the training consulting firm that I founded in 1989, invited Gene Kranz to keynote our client-only conference. Kranz was the mission control manager during the ill-fated Apollo 13 flight; his presentation included film clips about the Apollo program and its astronauts. These men were a collection of extreme individualists (top gun fighter and test pilots) who had learned to collaborate as a team, and to submerge their considerable egos in a common cause. Kranz' message was clear and it wasn't lost on the audience.

For law firms, popular culture provides additional messaging – not only about what a team is, and how team members must relate within the team – but about the kind of leadership that is possible in a environment governed by stress, and in a culture driven by centrifugal forces. While the movies offer us a number of leadership styles, the most interesting – because the most complex – are the positive examples. The villains are seldom interesting because, as leaders, they are one-dimensional.

Take James Cagney's hateful scow captain in *Mister Roberts*. His style is based on simple disrespect. He punishes by depriving his men of privileges, which means he's treating them just as a rather uncreative parent treats a recalcitrant child. He cannot, and will not, inspire them to do anything of value, because he doesn't see any value in them.

Tragically enough, we saw the logical and extreme result of such autocratic and disrespectful leadership in Vietnam. "Fragging" is a forgotten term in use during that war. It referred to the killing of American officers by their own men. It was more common than we could imagine. The business equivalent of fragging is when team members intentionally sabotage the team because they simply can't stand the leader.

By contrast, the men will move mountains for Mister Roberts, played by Henry Fonda, because they know he will do the same for them. As in most non-military professions, Mister Roberts is a *superior among peers*; the men sense that his authority is not willful or capricious, and that it is based solely on the fact that he has accepted his superior position as a matter of responsibility.

The value of our cinematic heritage for law firms struggling to identify leaders is in the variety of positive role models presented. A leader should have most of the attributes listed above, but the composite result can, from one **Client-Focused Team** to another, look very different. Consider:

Henry Fonda (again) in *Twelve Angry Men*. This is Socratic leadership at its most powerful. He doesn't ordain his vision. Again, leadership is a responsibility more than a privilege. Fonda doesn't seek power. He fills a void that has to be filled. He only asks that each member of his team (and a jury is indeed a team) look deep within themselves, and be as honest with themselves as possible. He trusts the team members to respond with their best. Not all can or will respond like that. In the movie, three characters remain unregenerate even though they do finally vote for acquittal.

William Shatner in *Star Trek*. The abiding fascination of Captain Kirk is that, as a starship commander, his power is formidable. But, to command that power, he must be demonstrably equitable, as the Star Fleet system doesn't tolerate Captain Queegs. Kirk happily accedes to, and relies on, the expertise of others. His authority represents a combination of the best qualities of those around him. He is a feeling man, but not as emotional as McCoy; he is intensely rational, but not as coldly logical as Spock. The leadership equation here is thus based on complementariness. His team members recognize themselves in him, but also see in him what they lack.

Robin Williams in *Dead Poets Society*. Like Fonda in *Twelve Angry Men*, this leadership style trusts to the team members; he allows them to discover themselves. Unlike Fonda, he is also exhortatory. He makes his value system eminently clear, and the fact that it is an iconoclastic style additionally appeals to young men who have been stifled in proprieties. Williams directly inspires in a way that Fonda does not. The Socratic Fonda leads in order to uncover the truth. The Dionysian Williams leads in order to liberate. The Fonda type tends to outlast the Williams type, since the Williams type is often a moving target in a hostile world.

Russell Crowe in *Gladiator*. No Roman leader can be weak or sentimental. But he can be fair, and the Gladiator is. He can be compassionate, and the Gladiator is. Crowe's leadership grows as he suffers, and the real test of it is his ability is – not to command as a general, when the men have no choice except to obey – to command when he returns as a former convict. At that point, his power is based on the quiet conviction which he radiates, and the almost certain knowledge on the part of his team members that he is right. They also know that he has paid his dues. He has undergone as many bad days as they have.

These are very different personalities, yet there are powerful connections, beginning with the leader's non-negotiable
respect for the team members. The leader succeeds in getting his
team members to do what they might not do on their own: acquit
an innocent man, read romantic poetry, risk their lives in another
galaxy or in the arena. For the most part, however, the key to
this success is not by coercing, but by inspiring team members to
reach within themselves for the strength to succeed.

Toward that end, we'd bet on Henry Fonda and William
Shatner any day! Contrast them to the typical leadership models
that are easily observed at law firms and other organizations:

The bean counters. Their total reliance on the numbers to
manage the firm is "timing the high jump". Numbers don't always reflect the reality of the challenges the people in the firm
face.

The distant ones. They may not disrespect you like the
captain in Mister Roberts. But they may not know your name or
your contributions.

The Narcissus. The team is just an extension of his or her
self-gratifying vision or will.

The autocrat. Occasionally the George C. Patton types
win the crucial battle. But Eisenhower knew enough to replace
Patton with Omar Bradley, "the soldier's general." Ike was positive it would make for a better, more stable global team, and he
was right.

In his best-selling *The Wisdom of Teams*, Jon Katzenbach
uses the phrase "leaderless teams". These teams motivate themselves because they have been led to do so. Once there is mutual
agreement on goals, the peer group takes over, and the leader
leads only by advising where his or her advice is needed. But
that is a point only a truly superior leader will ever reach.

Henry Fonda did not acquit the defendant in *Twelve Angry Men*. The jury did.

What Leaders Do

So you've found the ideal Henry Fonda to lead a **Client-Focused Team** targeting the biggest company in town, with some of the best litigators, corporate lawyers, and real estate lawyers in the firm volunteering for the team. Now what?

The first step is an orientation meeting – an especially important rite of passage, as it sends the message that the formation (or reformation) of the team represents a fresh start. Whatever else has been done to land the client in the past is important only as background. This is Day One of the campaign.

The meeting should last for one to two hours and cover:

- The role of the team leader
- The role of the team members
- Rules for working together

All data necessary for the team members to set their goals should be distributed at the meeting. For example, any available information on legal fees paid out by the company to other law firms is essential if the team is to get a handle on what it's really going after in terms of volume of new business.

It is important that the goals not only be specific, but that they are written down as well. True, there are myriad written documents (often expensive ones written by consultants) that get put on shelves and ignored in perpetuity. At the same time, the written word has a power of its own to command allegiance, especially among lawyers for whom it might have the implicit value of a contract.

Subsequent meetings will fill in the blanks. Circulate the agenda early for each meeting, so there can be no excuses for being unprepared or late.

During the early months of a team's existence, there is an especially acute need for the leader to communicate vision. It is important that leaders do so in different ways – not just speeches or memos or power-point presentations, but a combination of all of the above and more. By varying the communication media, the leader deepens and reinforces the message. Relying on just one approach can prove soporific. Team members won't say, "We've heard all that before" if they can hear it in different ways.

Teams fail because there are no established rules of behavior, because the members are constitutionally incapable of collaboration, because the leader is either coercive or indifferent. The resistance to collaboration often reflects a lack of experience: people who haven't worked much with others need to be taught how. It is a particular problem for lawyers, since the legal profession involves a great deal of solitary work, and, consciously or unconsciously, many lawyers prefer to work alone and are attracted to the law for just that reason.

One solution lies in how you staff the team. Identify lawyers who have worked successfully in teams before, and make them the majority shareholders in the **Client-Focused Team**. They will outnumber and out-vote the loners.

Teams fail because they are impatient. Part of the leadership role is to understand that it takes time to become a team. He or she needs to be alternatively supportive and decisive, to communicate what is still required to forge the team links, and to reassure members that the right progress is being made. At the same time, the leader must be listening hard to every team member for indications of success and failure.

Teams fail because they prefer to self-medicate when professional help is clearly required. The objective and experienced perspective is always valuable.

Teams fail because there is a disconnect between the team and firm management. The number of managing partners who would replace a majority of their practice group heads if they had their druthers is just astonishing. The team leader must have a viable relationship with key managers outside the team, and, by garnering positive feedback to team initiatives from those managers, further encourage team unity and resolve.

It Can Be Done

Law firms are culturally notorious. They are notorious because lawyers can be singularly self-absorbed – even in a marketplace like the current one, where competitive pressures demand a more collaborative approach to both client development and client retention. Yet nothing inspires like success, and many of our law firm clients that have seen the tangible results of these **Client-Focused Teams**.

Conclusion

Two facts are indisputable. One, collaborative teams succeed in generating more business than teams that are not collaborative. Two, great team leaders get their teams to accomplish things they could not do on their own, and they usually succeed at that, not by coercing, but by drawing out the inherent capabilities of their team members.

Unfortunately there's a third fact confronting us: the skills to lead **Client-Focused Teams** are not part of most lawyers' DNA. Yet we know what traits define effective leadership, and most firms may certainly find a requisite number of partners who, for whatever happy chance or circumstance, approximate that paradigm.

Alternatively, law firms that recognize a dearth of leadership potential in their own ranks can take steps to improve. How? Firms can institute leadership skills programs to inculcate the qualities of true leaders. Some firms have already done so, but they make their mistake by limiting attendance only to those senior partners they already see as their leaders. These **Client-Focused Teams** can serve as the incubator for developing future leaders. If you can inspire a team to do business development and like it you can probably lead the firm to greater wealth, financially and culturally.

The next great step is to share the wealth: Train junior partners in leadership skills. Train associates. The firms that do so soonest will own the future.

3

Just Say No:
When Law Firms Should NOT Partici-
pate In Beauty Contests

"Law firms must learn, not only how to effectively compete in a beauty contest, but also how to assess each beauty contest opportunity—and know when to simply decline to participate."

It's the defining moment in law firm marketing. Here's a professional caste called lawyers who, a decade ago, regarded any form of marketing as unseemly at best, demeaning at worst. The idea of going hat in hand to a prospective client—any prospective client—and competing with other law firms in a so-called "beauty contest," would have seemed absurd.

Now, after years of competitive wrangling, law firms are waiting in line at beauty contests for a chance to pitch their practices. These beauty contests have signaled the birth of a new era in the history of the legal profession, for at least four reasons.

First, the law firm is being asked to prove its very existence as a quality organization.

Second, the firm has to justify its staffing procedures, its billing rates, even the coherence of its work product in ways it would have thought unthinkable a few years ago.

Third, the firm has to be willing to compromise in areas, like pricing, that it once arrogantly deemed non-negotiable.

Fourth, the firm has to compete for its own business. Old client relationships are not only at risk, they're at risk in quasi-public settings! Like a middle manager in a downsized or acquired company who has to interview for his or her own job, law firms now must resell themselves to existing clients who may be indifferent to yesterday's accomplishments and the implicit commitments of the past.

In other words, beauty contests, more than any other phenomenon in today's competitive environment, demonstrates that *the client is in control.* Of course, they are in control. The very integrity of professional services is predicated on obsessive client service. In the client's view, the shift in control is a welcome alternative to the perceived arrogance and independence which too many law firms indulged a decade or so ago.

On the other hand, the shift in the client's favor has been so enormous that, it invites a certain disingenuousness on the part of many clients. Old clichés like "power corrupts" survive as clichés because they happen to be all too true. The apparent abuses of power by some clients are nowhere more evident than in how they set up and manage beauty contests. Law firms must learn, not only how to effectively compete in a beauty contest, but also how to assess each beauty contest opportunity—and know when to simply decline to participate.

Participation is voluntary (provided you remember that the "golden rule" applies: i.e., those that have the gold do unto others as they darn well please). Yet, in the current market, non-participation could seem to be a radical decision. It may give most law firms a queasy feeling to spurn the advances of the corporate buyer with rumors that they are too arrogant to compete. Maybe the buyers will start thinking you don't need or want new work!

30

My advice is to be bold and just say no—provided you know how to spot the tell-tale signs that reveal which beauty contests are dangerous wastes of time. In most such instances, clients are just looking for leverage. They've made up their minds to retain another firm. Any commitment you make to lower rates or lower costs gives them negotiating power with whomever they've already selected. In other words, you're being used.

Even worse, clients could divulge information in a beauty contest that will disqualify your firm from representing a competitor. Not only might you be conflicted out from handling a related transaction or litigation, you could be permanently disqualified from working for one or more companies on any matter.

Sounds paranoid? It happened a few years ago to one of the nation's ten largest firms. All the evidence suggests that a preliminary interview was a purposeful tactic used by the prospective client to make sure this great firm was put out of commission. By all accounts, it was a painful experience.

Here's a bit of general advice: approach each beauty contest as if its host were already a new client. Treat it like more like a marketing opportunity. Apply the same client intake process, replete with preliminary research and conflict monitoring, that the firm applies when any new representation walks in the door.

Even when you're relatively confident the firm is on safe ground, make sure that your lawyers talk hypothetically, during the beauty contest itself, both about the matters that the interviewing client intends to assign as well as any past or present related matters the firm is handling.

Few could hope to read the minds of many corporate legal buyers. Fortunately, there are red flags that indicate when a beauty contest is probably bogus. These signals are found in the wording of the request-for-proposal that initiates the beauty contest process, or in certain statements or actions by the client before and afterward.

In some cases, these red flags suggest the retention decision has already been made and that your chances are nil from the get-go. In other instances, the job might still be open, yet participation in the beauty contest could be injurious. In fact, the worst-case scenario is that you'll win the beauty contest and get the job, with a client who instinctively looks at you like an adversary.

If I were a managing partner or practice group head, I'd memorize these signals:

➤ *Arm's-length client.* Any refusal on the part of general counsel or whoever makes the final retention decision to meet directly with key law firm representatives *beforehand* is generally a sign they are not serious.

Clients complain, when law firms don't send the right lawyers to a beauty contest. If, for example, a marketing partner shows up without the practice group head who'll be handling the work that's up for grabs, it shows less than complete seriousness on the part of the seller.

That sword certainly cuts both ways. If the person who's got the actual clout to hire you isn't there, you're sitting in the wrong room. That person is probably talking at that very moment to the firm that *will* be hired.

➤ *Impersonal communications.* This is a significant variation on the arm's-length client. If you're in serious contention, particularly for a major litigation or transaction—and certainly if you're in a beauty contest that will consolidate all the client's work among a greatly reduced number of law firms—the prospective client couldn't possibly be unwilling to personally meet with you at any time to discuss his or her legal needs.

Remember, for most types of representations decided at beauty contests, the client will wind up virtually living with outside counsel for the duration. Clients usually know this. It is in their obvious self-interest to get to know you as closely as possible. If they're only willing to communicate by mail, they're pulling your chain.

➤ *Overemphasis on rates.* Look carefully at the RFP, or try to get some prior sense of what the client wants you to talk about most in your presentation. If it's fees and price, if there's a strong focus on hourly rates, you may want to sit this one out. They're likely shopping price in order to squeeze their current counsel.

As an issue in a beauty contest, the cost of legal services is second to none in importance for everyone. But there's a big difference between *cost* and *rates* per hour. Discussions about cost are creative and freewheeling. They test flexibility on both sides. They test the seller's willingness to help the buyer save money without deleterious effect on the seller. They test the buyer's willingness to formulate cost-effective schedules that still provide incentives for the seller to do a good job.

Rates are one part of the cost discussion. As soon as you see they're the only part, go home and mow the lawn.

➤ *Unattainable goals.* Here's another example of bad faith financial negotiation. The client is insisting on budgets that cannot possibly be sustained, or asking for write-downs that would be burdensome even to the most cost-efficient law firms.

One of two things is happening when clients bargain for the impossible. It could be another give-away that the decision about whom to hire has already been made, and that you're being used as a bargaining tool.

Or, even worse, the client actually wants the firm eventually hired to pledge itself to undoable standards. Maybe you'll kill yourself trying to stay within the unrealistic cost parameters. The client still saves a bundle in legal fees even if you fall short of the original projections. Or, maybe you won't come anywhere near meeting the goals. That irrevocably poisons the water between you and the client. But the buyer then poses as the disappointed party and thus maintains a psychological advantage.

Most law firms would not agree to impracticable budget or performance goals, but I'd further advise a firm to walk away from any beauty contest where the clients begin by postulating impossible cost restraints, even if they're only doing so as a negotiating ploy. The fact is, you deserve more good faith than that. Most of the corporate clients you should want to be representing are as concerned about your economics as you are, because they know your financial survival is also in their best interest.

The clients whose business is worth competing for look at you the same way you look at the vendors who supply your litigation support software or keep your networks up and running. If they go broke, you could too. Clients who'd bargain law firms to the brink aren't worth representing unless, of course, you're absolutely desperate for another client.

➢ *Artificial proposal or bid deadlines.* Overly specific deadlines are usually a sign the client is just gathering market data to use in negotiations with someone else. ASAP deadlines are real red flags. Such deadlines severely limit a law firm's capacity to be competitive.

The client probably knows this, but doesn't care. After all, the client doesn't need a firm that's not really in the running to be competitive.

➢ *No performance standards for selection.* Look carefully at the RFP. If there is no statement somewhere in it, or if you can't get a thoughtful response from the company, as to how the winner will be chosen, then it's because there probably won't be a winner.

Ideally, there should be two types of provisions clearly communicated by the client. First, the RFP should articulate criteria for winning: depth in specific practice areas, willingness to adhere to the budget, willingness to accept a regular management review by the client, ability to work with local counsel, etc. A clear report card for performance is mutually beneficial.

Also, the client should be willing to disclose verbally or in writing who specifically is making the retention decision, what sort of follow-up or further effort after the beauty contest could help candidates influence the final decision, and when the decision will be made. This is all basic courtesy, folks. If they're not basically courteous, then you should basically not be interested.

➤ *No oral presentations.* Here, your written response to the RFP is decisive, too much so. The beauty contest itself—if there actually is one—becomes a Kafkaesque interrogation in which the client picks out specific points from the RFP and asks respondents generally close-ended questions. It's tantamount to a corporate MRI in which a law firm is the patient with absolutely no room to move.

This approach is particularly suspect since informed retention decisions obviously depend on the most expansive possible verbal discussion. The client ought at some point, either in the RFP or in follow-up communications, to indicate when and where law firms under consideration will have opportunities for such ample dialogue.

Law firms that see too many of these red flags flying may decide they really need to compete in substantially fewer beauty contests—if any at all! Yet, marketing is an art that requires constant refinement, and law firms shouldn't necessarily neglect opportunities for practice. In other words, there's at least one reason to participate even when one or more of the above signs convince you the beauty contest is a shell game, and that's because you need the experience.

There's another good reason to compete in a rigged beauty contest, albeit a depressing reason. Your own client is bidding out the work you've been doing because new management wants a change, or at least wants to see what's out there. The decision to dump the firm may already be irreversible, yet you still have to prepare a presentation and take your best shot. It's your client, after all, until you hear otherwise.

Not just as a training exercise, beauty contests may help firms market themselves irrespective of their chances of winning the main event. You may, for example, do such a good job in your presentation that the client will retain you for a choice piece of the work—even when there had been no original intention of assigning it elsewhere than to the company's current and primary firm.

Second, most beauty contests offer an ideal opportunity to get the word out on a new service, or a new practice group, or a prominent partner who's just lateraled in. We hear no end of stories about corporate clients surprised, and very interested, to learn that a firm is strong in an area that has nothing to do with the competition at hand.

Some of the clients who hold beauty contests will never meet you half way. But among the others, there are some who, while they are dragging firms through beauty contests they can't win, are still open-minded enough and shrewd enough to pay close attention to everyone who passes through. With these clients, we ought to redefine the premise. Their beauty contests aren't totally bogus; they're simply longer-term opportunities than the original RFP might have suggested.

The point is, it's still worth competing for their work even if the decision on immediate retention has already been made. Firms get great air time this way, and a chance to be a bona fide front-runner the next time the client goes shopping.

Lawyers have to get over the old bugaboo of valuing a marketing effort only if it leads directly to new business. The most lucrative marketing is longer-term than that, and a beauty contest that's not winnable today may be the best case in point. The key is to clearly define what you want, on a prospective client-by-client basis, and to at least realize that every RFP is an investment opportunity.

Invest wisely!

Ten Ideas On How To Win
Competitive Business Opportunities
or
Secrets From "Beauty Contest" Winners

"Instead of treating business competitions with a serious, studied and planned approach, lawyers and firms underrespond because they see the requisite non-billable time as an unproductive intrusion into their lawyering activities."

Most law firm beauty contests are won or lost well before the main event -- during the preparation phase (or lack of it, as the case may be). These competitive business opportunities take some preparation, however, and therein lies the problem. Instead of treating business competitions with a serious, studied and planned approach, lawyers and firms underrespond because they see the requisite non-billable time as an unproductive intrusion into their lawyering activities. Resentment to competitive bids is hardly a winning strategy.

Your biggest challenge as a marketing director will be to convince your lawyers that RFPs and competitive business presentations are an investment and should be entered into with the attitude, enthusiasm and prospect of profitability. The following suggestions will help. They are not just our ideas; they come from the collective wisdom and experience of over 50 marketing directors who have competed in several hundred presentations and proposals over the last eight years.

1. Compete to win. Or don't compete. Treat the opportunity the same way you would a jury trial with a contingency fee equal to the fees that will arise out of the opportunity. Prepare your proposal and oral presentation as you would prepare the brief or the opening argument to the jury. Your lawyers should think about the strategy for winning, the informational content of the proposal and the presentation, the mechanics of the oral presentations and who will deliver their message. If it's not worth preparing for, it's not worth entering. You not only lose, but also leave a tarnished business card.

2. Know the "enemy." Beauty contests are about what the judges think is beautiful, not how beautiful you think you are. They probably already know how large the firm is, how many offices and lawyers there are, and so forth. Clients want to know that you understand their problems and are capable of providing solutions. They will generally be impressed if you make a pre-bid needs assessment visit. If your lawyers complain about the time commitment, reassure them that they need to do this only in those situations they want to win. An added benefit of a pre-bid needs assessment visit is that you are likely to discover early on if the process is a sham -- say, a strategy by the prospect to eliminate competition by way of creating conflicts; and you can politely decline to participate and focus on better opportunities.

3. Clients want lawyers, not resumes. Legal technicians are a dime a dozen. Whatever the RFP says, most prospects are also looking for trusted counselors and trust cannot be earned in a presentation but rapport can; and trust follows from rapport. The pre-bid needs assessment visit will show your interest and commitment, and identify potential points of rapport for the next meeting or presentation.

As for the technical discussion of the client's needs, you will need to help your lawyers talk about solutions -- which is what the client's looking for -- and not problems -- which is what your lawyers enjoy. Too often lawyers get trapped in discussing the transaction or litigation in negative terms -- i.e. legal problems or legal obstacles -- rather than discussing the outcome the client wants. A transaction may appeal to the lawyers as cutting edge legal theory, and they may get caught up in the elegance and the fun of working on the problem. The client, meanwhile is left behind pondering.

4. Have one central message or theme, linked to the client. If "Quality is Job 1" to the client, how does your firm plan to integrate that credo to the relationship and provide seamless, quality service?

Lawyers tend to reject themes or messages as superficial and too commercial -- something that advertising types might concoct. Your lawyers may feel that any attempt to incorporate themes or messages into their presentation or proposal will be viewed with disdain and smacks of Madison Avenue and, therefore, look unprofessional. Your job is to convince them that this is not about what makes them comfortable, but what matters to the prospect. Clients react favorably to the use of their products, services and business messages in presentations or proposals.

5. Set the selection criteria. In many cases, the prospect does not establish the selection criteria until during or after the presentations. Provided you are suitably subtle, you can help shape the selection criteria. If you do, nature will take its course, and you will inevitably be establishing criteria that best conform to your strengths. For example, in suggesting to the buyers that they may need to look carefully at all the options, some of those options they may not have considered should be areas of expertise that you or your firm possess. Mark McConnack, the lawyer, sports agent, author and lecturer, pointed out recently that he had bought things when someone had helped him recognize a need he had not previously considered. There is no reason for not submitting an actual list of criteria during the oral presentation, provided you are reasonably certain it tracks the clients' major needs, and you get agreement early on.

6. Talk about value not about price. Few people who've read The Grapes of Wrath can forget the scene where the growers line the workers up and tell them to take a step forward if they want a job for 30 cents a day; then ask those who've stepped forward to take another step if they want a job for 25 cents a day and so on until they get the number they need at 10 cents a day -- essentially playing the workers off against each other. This is where your lawyers will eventually be if they focus on price instead of value -- the value they bring to the transaction. Price becomes a determining factor when you have failed to differentiate yourself in a way the prospect can value. When there are substitutes available, the bidding starts.

7. Talk, write and present the way they do. Whenever possible, use the prospective client's business jargon and product terminology, and present your solutions in the same manner as they present to themselves internally. Business-speak is an art that can help you seem more like them and reduces the "we vs. they" barrier. Tailoring your message and the medium of presentation can make your buyer feel comfortable that you are not "outsiders." And if you plan to use technology and presentation graphics, make sure you are not using a competitor's product. (And don't absent-mindedly ask for a Coke during a presentation to Pepsi; don't Fed-X a proposal to DHL; etc.)

8. Be on time. Since a prospect cannot really know you, it has no choice but to base inordinate weight on stats. Every contact with the issuer is an opportunity to create impressions.

Beating the deadline for the submission of the written RFP may create the impression of responsiveness. Showing up 15 minutes early for the oral presentation and staying within the allotted time will show that you are punctual and organized. And never try to blame your tardiness on another important client engagement. What the client will hear is "another client, not important." And never fail to respond or show up for the presentation without offering a cogent business reason why you've declined to participate.

9. Make the business case on why -- and whether - you should be hired. Determine for yourself -- and be able to articulate clearly -- how a prospective client in the situation at hand will benefit by, first, hiring a law firm and, second, hiring your law firm. That will get you deep inside their business mind, and get you much farther than arguing why they should hire you instead of the other guy. Most businesses have standard models to justify the cost of a project. Some use strict ROI (return on investment) models; others use return on net assets or return on stockholder equity; others have well developed home-grown techniques. Ask and you shall receive. Ask the decisionmaker which models they are using to cost-justify spending the money. If you don't have exact data, get the buyers to agree that your educated guesses are sufficient.

10. Act like their partner not like a vendor. The shift to the preferred supplier model and partnering with outside sources of supply is now the norm in sophisticated businesses. The legal press, business journals and the general press are reporting consolidation by the buyers to fewer law firms. The RFPs are calling for partnering with their outside counsel. Partnering is codeword for a lot of different relationships with outside counsel. The best way to approach partnering is to look at how the prospective client works with outside resources in other parts of their business. Focus the potential relationship on their definitions not yours.

41

Marketing Director's Opportunity

If you ever wondered what your marketing mission or skills were good for in a den of cynics and marketing skeptics, then the RFP and the competitive business presentation is an opportunity to help. Most of the lawyers we talk with are annoyed that they have to waste billable time to compete for work that they deserve. The reality in the market is that competition for work in what is now a deregulated profession is good. Good for the clients, good for the public at large and great for those firms not in marketing denial. Your mission as a marketing director is to create the positive mind set amongst your lawyers and help them compete effectively.

If your lawyers are poorly prepared, unrehearsed and approach the opportunity with a negative attitude, then you need only to point out that their competition is probably in about the same dismal state! We have seen the most incompetent and unconscious lawyers at marketing rise to the occasion as a result of the marketing director's ability to help them recognize the need to win and avoid committing marketing malpractice.

This article was featured in the October 1996 issue of NALFMA's *Law Marketing Exchange* and the August 26, 1996 edition of *Texas Lawyer*.

5

20 Questions You Should Ask
Current and Prospective Clients

"Clients don't want a sales pitch, and they don't need to be told about your lawyering skills. They probably assume you're good at what you do, or you wouldn't have gotten this far."

Note: This article has been published in several publications since authoring it in 1990. This version was updated in April 2006.

You've been representing your client for some time. They are aware of your expertise. They have seen your firm's brochures, attended the firm's seminar last month, are familiar with your website, and have received the firm's newsletter. You think there is potential for more business. You've invited the CEO or general counsel to lunch, presumably to develop more business by trying to cross-sell the rest of your firm.

You may have invited a partner from your firm to go along. The partner's role may be that of a potential new practice area opportunist or as a sympathizer if the "cross-selling" lunch craters. Now the real challenge begins: What are you going to say at lunch?

Here's where rainmaking often turns into drought. Here, lawyers inexperienced in business development often make the crucial mistake of assuming that they're the ones who are supposed to do all the talking. For lack of anything better to do, they start their "sales pitch." Or they try to convince clients or prospective clients that the firm has a number of good lawyers who can help them. Or more likely, they start with a small talk as their way of trying to build rapport. The first 45 minutes of the lunch focuses on the U.S. Open, sports, the weather or subject matter that borders on the trivial, and often, inappropriately personal.

But clients and prospective clients don't want a poorly thought out sales pitch, and they don't need to be told about your lawyering skills. They probably assume you're good at what you do, or you wouldn't have gotten this far. And they certainly don't want personal, small talk. They're as busy as you are.

What they want is to feel comfortable with you as a professional, and to see where you and your firm might fit in with their **business objectives**. To make them comfortable, get them to talk about themselves and their business objectives. Your efforts should focus on listening to their responses. The more they talk, the more you'll learn. And the more you learn, the more natural the process becomes. In business development, information is always power - because it means knowing what they need.

If lawyers need to develop more business, then knowing more about the buyer's business is what great business development is all about. Knowing what to ask and how to ask is an art and a science. These 20 questions are broad enough to apply to most types of clients - both current and prospective - yet specific enough to elicit the concrete information essential for effective business development.

Many of their questions seem to target new clients. But it is surprising how much lawyers don't know about the clients they've been serving for years. If those lawyers took the time to learn, they'd find there's substantial business going elsewhere which, with a little effort, could be kept in the family.

Asking clients about themselves will uncover opportunities that require not just your expertise, but your partners' as well. It means long-term client relationships and long-term profit - not just one matter today that won't pay any bills tomorrow.

Long-term is the key. When they hear you asking about their plans three to five years hence, they begin to think of you as a 30-year ally. Don't worry about asking new clients direct questions. This is information they tell their brokers, their PR staffs, the stockholders, the press and others in the business world. And they certainly want to tell you, because they want to *trust* their lawyers. They have critical business information they need to share with their lawyers.

Likewise, current clients will appreciate your interest. They may even realize that such expert listening is the crux of delivering quality legal services. These questions assume that these meetings are with the decision-makers, including business executives, general counsel or the legal department.

First, here are a few basic rules:

➢ You cannot and should not try to "sell" legal services to unwilling buyers. You should not try to close the business at the first available lull in the conversation. Avoid the "sales pitch," as they may not be in the "catching" mode.

➢ Never put them on the defensive. Don't use the same style of questioning you'd use in a deposition or while cross-examining a hostile witness. This should be a win-win. The better they feel about talking now, the better they'll feel about hiring you later. Let them be the ones to bring up sensitive or painful matters. Try to avoid the "why" questions, which are likely to carry a judgmental tone. It's empathy and rapport that you're after.

➢ Make all your questions as open-ended as possible. A "yes" or "no" answer will seldom do you any good. Phrase questions in such a way as to give them the opportunity to supply as much information as possible.

> Don't feel you need to respond to everything they tell you. Much of what they say should be filed away, for future use at a more appropriate moment. Silence can help build informational savings accounts.

> As previously mentioned, do your preliminary research. They want to tell you about themselves and their needs, but they'll also appreciate the respect you show when you take the trouble to learn as much about them as you can. Use public data bases, newspaper articles and the client's own publications as sources. Give those stockbrokers that call you daily some homework; and ask them to do research on your behalf!

The needs-analysis process follows its own course and cannot be rigidly encapsulated. Ideally, you may want to start by asking general questions about their business: what they manufacture, sell and to whom. There's nothing they'd rather talk about. Then explore how they've structured their organizations. Finally, focus on their legal needs: how they've met those needs in the past and intend to do so in the future.

Here are the important questions:

1. What do you want your organization to look like in one year, two years or five years?

This question is a good opener, because it allows buyers to begin talking about any aspect of their business they choose. But you also have your own tactical reason for asking it, which is to determine if they've formulated a strategic plan and, if so, what that plan involves.

Now is the time to listen and learn, not promote. But if the buyer mentions, for instance, international growth as a part of the strategy, you may have spotted a great opportunity right off the bat, assuming you or your firm has expertise in that area.

Asking about strategic planning tells you something else as well. It tells you what kind of self-knowledge they have. Do they have a specific vision of what they want for themselves, or are they playing the field, reacting to events and market developments as they happen? Getting a feel for them in this way may tell you volumes about how they deal with every other aspect of their business, including hiring lawyers.

How long have they been in business? It's an obvious question, but don't forget to ask it if you don't already know. Mature businesses often have more experience with outside counsel, and many of their legal problems have already been resolved. With start-ups, the needs-analysis process has a completely different texture. You may need to explore fundamental questions, like setting up ESOPs or going public, that the buyer may not have thought through yet.

2. When and where do you plan to open new offices or plants?

This seemingly innocuous question is more than just a further refinement of the strategic planning issue. It will help you focus on a whole range of possible legal services, from real estate and lease negotiations to benefits planning for new staffs. In addition, it's information that will give you a real sense of just how aggressive and confident the buyer is. It's one thing to talk about a strategic plan. It's another thing to state boldly, "We intend to open 10 new branches in the next two years."

3. What new products, services or major changes are you anticipating?

What if a retailer decides they want to offer a discount brokerage service? Suddenly there's a whole range of legal expertise that you and your firm may have, but that you had no idea that they would ever have this particular need. And they may have no idea you feature a securities practice. Here, the opportunity speaks for itself - thunderously.

4. What kind of research and development do you see as necessary for you to meet your strategic objectives?

Legal counsel is itself a form of R&D, particularly where they will be breaking new ground. As they talk more about their plans - how much they plan to invest, and the kind of research they'll be doing - you may even get a glimpse of your own future: the practice areas you'll need to develop to be at the cutting edge five or ten years down the road.

5. What is the profile of your typical customer?

Getting a sense of who their customers are may help you determine how they themselves behave as customers. Are their buyers highly sophisticated and demanding, and to what extent? If so, they may want to see some evidence that you also treat your clients as peers.

Understanding how they market their products or services will naturally give you some clues as to how you should be approaching them. If they de-emphasize the direct pitch, maybe you should, too. But, there's another reason to explore their marketing approach. How they structure their sales force, whether it's decentralized or pyramidal, and the quota pressures under which those salespeople operate, will give you crucial insights into their culture. What the company expects from its district managers, it may also expect from you.

6. What are your employee relations concerns?

How they manage their sales force leads to a broader issue: how they manage their entire work force. This line of inquiry will strengthen your sense of their culture and its impact on their legal needs. Is it a paternalistic milieu, or a demanding and confrontational one?

Querying their concerns here also will help accomplish two other basic objectives. First, it will indicate current or future labor/employee problems: collective bargaining, wrongful discharge, benefits planning, etc. Second, it will increase their comfort level with you. Whether they are a closely-held businesses or Fortune 500 giants, there's nothing they fret about more, and nothing they'd rather talk over with a lawyer.

48

7. Who are your main competitors?

Here's another opportunity to get a sense of the business climate in which they are operating. Where there's an ongoing survival struggle with competitors, there are myriad legal issues, like commercial litigation, that the decisionmaker may not yet be pondering but ought to. Conversely, less intense competitive environments may direct the client dialogue elsewhere.

8. What has the financial climate been like for your business?

Use care here. This is information you need to have, but the question must be presented in as non-threatening a way as possible. You don't want to put anyone on the defensive. And you certainly don't want them thinking you're worried about who's going to pay the bill.

You're really trying to accomplish something very different. If they are in distress, they may want to think about spinning off a division, or even tapping your or your firm's bankruptcy expertise. Or perhaps you will want eventually to suggest custom-designed billing methods. You may even want to mention that you have helped other companies under the gun.

Once you have a sense of where they are in the marketplace, shift the focus somewhat. Find out what makes them tick.

9. How are you organized, what does your organization chart look like, and who are the key executives?

You're really trying to gauge the organization's level of complexity. Is it a flat organization or hierarchal? Are there dozens of subsidiaries, or is it a one-cell organism? You don't necessarily need the whole organization chart, just enough information to know with whom you're dealing. The names of the key executives are important at this juncture. You may never actually meet, say, the CFO, but you certainly don't want to sound ignorant later if that person's name comes up.

You may, for example, uncover reporting relationships between their divisions or subsidiaries that you never suspected.

10. How are decisions made, and who are the decision-makers?

Here, you're fleshing out the political underpinnings of the organizational setup. How bureaucratic is it? How autocratic? How many meetings will be needed before decisions, including retention decisions, are made? How efficiently are legal counsel implemented? For lawyers in particular, it's vital to know who specifically makes the decisions. Is there a general counsel? If not, it may be advisable to minimize legal jargon in the face-to-face needs-analysis process.

11. What is the leadership style here?

This question will give them an opportunity to provide a wealth of insight into the personalities of the key players. Get a sense of those people before you meet them. You may learn that the leadership style emphasizes consensus-building. That's a cue to suggest setting up other meetings with as many of those important team players as possible. Even brief introductions are useful. The more decision-makers you meet, the more opportunities open up.

12. Is there a legal department, how is it organized, and what is it's role?

Many sophisticated users of legal services have legal departments. The role of the legal department and its officers vary widely. Obviously, you need to know, but be careful here. The general counsel may be out of the decision-making loop altogether. Let them describe the role of their legal department and draw your own conclusions. But ask to meet the members of the legal department in any event. There's no point in alienating your in-house counterparts.

13. What do you see outside counsel accomplishing for you or your organization?

Again, the question is broad enough so that it's the clients who supply the essential information. Let them tell you what they want to buy, not just react to what you assume they need. They state their needs. YOU decide if you can fill them.

14. What recent uncertainties are affecting your business, or what changes of any sort have particularly concerned you recently?

They have something on their minds, otherwise they wouldn't be talking to a lawyer. Some of them may want to jump right in and tell you about a serious problem that's been keeping them awake at night. Others will prefer to talk about bewildering regulatory, political or market changes. But even generalities will highlight what they need from you today, as well as how you might be solving their other problems tomorrow and the day after tomorrow.

You're now on the verge of making an absolutely crucial determination: Does this person want proactive counseling or crisis management? You're not going to use the same tone of voice with a client who wants you to co-pilot long-range business strategy that you'd use for someone who needs you as a safety net. To know which tone of voice will make them most comfortable, listen carefully to the tone they use with you.

15. What sort of legal services are you currently using, and do you expect any changes?

Perhaps they've been relying on outside counsel for, say, garden variety tax work or ERISA. If so, ask yourself why they're talking to you now. Maybe some new and critical situation is in the offing, and they feel the need to shop around. Or perhaps they're just dissatisfied with their current counsel and are looking to turn everything over to another firm.

This line of inquiry is also helpful because you'll be able to compare their current legal needs with the services they're now buying. Something may well be missing on the service end. With new or first-time buyers, there may be particularly glaring omissions. With long-term clients, watch for certain recurring patterns. Some of them may be turning to Firm X for, say, tax work, and to Firm Y for litigation. Do they even know that many firms offer the best of both? One-stop shopping is a powerful lure for most clients and prospective clients. Consolidating to fewer and fewer outside firms has been the most compelling "one-stop-shopping" trend in recent history.

For less sophisticated buyers, modify the questions. Ask them to imagine the best-case lawyer/client scenarios, as well as the worst.

16. What do you like about what other firms do, and what do you wish they would do differently?

Learn from your competitors' mistakes without attacking them directly. In fact, never make negative comments about your competitors. It reflects on the judgement of the buyer! Identify where they've fallen short in order to determine where you'll need to do better. It's helpful to find out who those other firms are, because they're likely to continue to compete with you for future work. The buyer may mention their names without your having to ask. This could turn out to be the most important question about your opportunity to replace competition.

17. How much detail do you like to get from your lawyers?

Here is where you can get a real picture of their legal environment, and how much knowledge of the law they're bringing to the table. That knowledge will have a direct impact on your business development efforts. They may not be interested in hearing about all the details of your most recent case and aren't likely to appreciate your trying to dazzle them with displays of esoteric legalese.

By the same token, if they demand line and verse on every deal, they may well expect to be talking shop before they hire anyone. Incidentally, if they take pride in their legal knowledge, they probably have invested power in their general counsel, at least in determining which firms get what business.

18. How do you perceive our firm in particular?

You should be listening here to two things. First, what is it that has interested them enough to consider hiring you? Is it a particular practice area or your firm's overall reputation? Define that strength and, whatever it is, reinforce it in your discussions.

But listen, too, for what even the most admiring are not perceiving. Remember, you're trying to build a long-term relationship. That means going beyond the one or two areas of expertise that they have seen fit to mention.

19. What criteria do you use in selecting lawyers? What makes a good lawyer?

A good lawyer may be variously defined as someone who wins cases, returns phone calls, respects in-house counsel or keeps costs down. Sometimes they have no particular impression of you or your firm, one way or another. They may just be spreading their nets, talking to as many lawyers as possible. So don't guess what they're looking for. Ask them.

20. How does your budgeting for legal services compare to what you spend on other resources?

Get a sense of the cost pressures beleaguering them. Sophisticated buyers aren't looking for bargain-basement rates, but they are attracted to lawyers who are sensitive to their need to stay within reasonable limits. Again, the main issue is their comfort level. They're going to want to know that you're someone they can deal with.

At this point you probably have developed a sense of the organization's operating environment, the personalities and their decision-making styles.

Any number of things might happen next. You may meet with other key executives. Or you will now begin preparing the formal presentation, written or verbal or both. With such myriad data now in hand, you can tailor that next step to their unique situation. You've substantially reduced the distance between you and built or enhanced the relationship.

Many lawyers don't reach this stage in a relationship, even with their established clients. Such relationships are built on trust, and trust is generally built on understanding and face-to-face communication. Asking relevant questions builds trust, and people give business to people they **trust**. Clients learn more about trusting lawyers and law firms from face-to-face meetings than any other source.

Too often, lawyers inexperienced in client relationship-building and business development squander business development opportunities. The sad part is that the decisionmakers may become permanently turned off to the lawyer's amateurish efforts. This could result in a loss of trust in their current lawyer. They will be reluctant to share information if they perceive that they will get a non-stop sales pitch. Avoid the premature "sales pitch," as it could have disastrous long-term implications for current and prospective client relationships.

The last question you may want to ask is the one that will lead to a commitment. Building relationships is a process, and one in which clients and prospective clients themselves participate. So ask your client or prospective client for help in determining what the next step might be rather than begging for the business using antique "closing" techniques.

6

It's The Client, Stupid

How to Avoid Marketing Malpractice With Large Key Clients.

"Does the firm have client relationship managers in place for each of our key clients? Is there a written plan in place for each key client that defines how the firm plans to retain and service the client?"

The bad news is that most law firms are marketing to the wrong people. The good news is that the solution is so simple that it was best stated by my dentist, George Olds: "Floss only those teeth you want to keep."

If the link between dentistry and marketing is not immediately apparent, the moral is this: if you take care of what you have, you can avoid painful, expensive replacement procedures.

In most law firms, 20 percent of the clients produce 80 percent of the revenue. Yet they typically receive a minuscule portion of the firm's marketing attention. Client retention is regarded as something outside the boundaries of marketing, and as only a minor factor in compensation. But increased competition, eroding client loyalty, "partnering" and a slew of other factors have made that an increasingly suicidal equation.

Willie Sutton may not be a proper role model, but he knew where the money was. Law firms, on the other hand, seem compelled to focus their limited marketing time and resources on where the money isn't -- dispatching hit teams all over the place to give new business pitches to prospective clients most of which will not pan out.

To be sure, natural attrition and other factors mandate that a firm keep looking for opportunities with new clients. But it's far more important to retain current clients. This is difficult for most firms to comprehend; that is, until a major client defects -- or fades away. Then they realize not only how much of their revenue the client represented, but also the incredible amount of additional time and resources must be devoted just to try to get back to where they were in revenues.

Why do firms lose these clients? Formal surveys point to how the client was treated by various members of the firm, i.e., poor service or neglect. Most well-established client relationships can sustain a litigation loss or a matter that exceeded the client's perception of cost; but not poor service in the form of missed client deadlines, phone calls not returned promptly and other acts of marketing negligence. Often, the loss of a client is due not to a single catastrophic event but to a cumulative series of "little murders" committed by partners. If clients do look for new outside counsel because of mismanaged relationships or neglect, then survival demands a strong key client relationship management program. The immediate and long-term mission of the program is client retention. Managing partners should ask the following questions:

- Does the firm have client relationship managers in place for each of our key clients?
- Is there a well-defined team in place that services each of these key clients?
- Does the team meet frequently to develop client retention or business development strategies?

- Is there a <u>written</u> plan in place for each key client that defines how the firm plans to retain and service the client?
- Do we conduct client opinion surveys of our key clients to get feedback on how our firm is performing?
- Is the client relationship manager accountable to the firm for increasing the client's satisfaction with our firm?
- Does the firm track -- by practice areas and potential practice areas -- opportunities for these clients?
- Does the firm hold internal review meetings to determine if the client managers and the teams are meeting the firm's objectives for these clients?

If the answer is "<u>no</u>" to most of these questions, then there is the chance that the key clients of the firm are not being well-managed and these clients are susceptible to competitive overtures. Leaving these key client relationships unmanaged is likely to result in client defections, either partial or complete, especially if competition is actively marketing to your key clients.

The single biggest threat to your firm's business is other law firms in your region, national firms and in large U.S. cities, the foreign-based law firms. However, competition for these large key clients may come from sources other than law firms. Contract lawyers hired as temporary in-house counsel may be, and frequently are, less expensive than outside law firms. Newly created research factories that turn out opinions on various legal issues may replace work traditionally done by your firm's associates. The client may elect to keep the work in-house. Frequently, the client may create a new position--tax manager; in-house human resources manager; or environmental consultant--that reduces the outside law firm's opportunity.

Another trend that may also cause a firm to lose business is the move by clients to consolidate to fewer outside law firms. This trend is reflected in the recent rash of RFPs (Request For Proposals) and beauty contests where the incumbent firms are being asked to rebid the relationship and a formal bidding process is used. The consolidation to fewer outside firms increases the client's needs to rely on more lawyers of the firm and should be viewed as an opportunity to create a client-focused team. These new "partnering" relationships are consistent with corporate America's trend toward downsizing and consolidating to fewer, more preferred suppliers, a benefit of the work of Dr. Edward Deming and TQM in the 1980s. The firm will need hard facts to understand these trends, the potential client defections and competitive exposures.

How To Analyze Key Client Relationships

The best way to begin the analysis is to create a computer spreadsheet of the top 150 clients on one axis and use the practice areas of the firm as the categories on the other coordinate. In each cell, show the revenue for clients by entering the fees collected yearly. This simple and powerful report shows which practice areas the client has been using, the overall fees collected annually, practice areas not utilized at all and finally, the variations year-to-year in revenue by practice area. To further refine this spreadsheet, it may be necessary to include more detail. An analysis of the client's organization is helpful. For example, the client may have in-house lawyers assigned to product divisions or geographic locations. Each division or location may have broad-ranging legal needs. The spreadsheet analysis may have to include both the overall company and each division. Also, practice areas of the firm may overlap as a real estate transaction may also involve environmental issues. Start with a simple system and move to the more complex later. By analyzing the various practice areas' revenues or lack of revenues, you may be able to pinpoint a potential client relationship problem. Once this information is collected and analyzed, it should be circulated to the designated client relationship manager. Ask the client manager a series of probing questions to understand why and where the revenues are coming from.

Who Are These Client Relationship Managers (CRM) and How Are They Selected?

The CRM selection process will need to be clear, open and carefully defined by firm's management to avoid the appearance of favoritism or politics. It is important that the client manager's role be one of an ombudsman and not an owner of the client. Select the person who will get best results for the client and the firm. Simply, that means taking the high road: Who will "play" best with the client? Who do they trust? Who at the firm makes them feel secure that their best interests are being looked after? In most firms, this process has a strong political content and even in the 90s lawyers continue to guard *their clients* jealously and may avoid exposing *their clients* to this approach. However, the alternative is to leave key client relationships unmanaged and, thus, fail to focus the firm's marketing resources on the retention of key clients of the firm. Client retention is typically undermanaged or overlooked in most firms.

Role of the Client Relationship Manager (CRM)

The goals of the Client Relationship Manager are to increase the client's satisfaction with the law firm, expand or retain the business that the firm does with the client and eventually increase profitability. In short, make an effort to develop the relationship between the firm and the client's organization. Although these relationships are typically built from a singular contact, the most profitable and enduring client relationships result from a complete network of contacts that yield business and opportunities for both the firm and the client's organization. The time the CRM spends as a CRM is typically non-billable. A business case for the investment of non-billable time can be made based on increased profitability due to key client retention.

The CRM should constantly focus the team on its goals, provide new vision and direction when the client shifts its strategy or responds to market forces. The CRM should motivate the team with positive feedback, keep goals and tasks relevant, select appropriate new team members, establish a sense of urgency and present new information. Most importantly, the CRM needs to maintain credibility with the client and the team by doing real legal work. The CRM should be accountable in a formal way to the firm for the overall state of the relationship.

The client relationship manager and the team should be responsible for forecasting potential revenue to ensure that the firm identifies the resources that are needed to meet the client's demands. Typically, sophisticated clients have done these same economic projections in the form of in-house legal budgets. In many firms, the CRM assists the client in preparing annual legal budget projections. The CRM needs to understand the client's business well enough to assist in identifying legal strategies and how to integrate legal services into the business to help in the budgeting process.

The CRM should serve as the focal point as both the client and the firm identify the appropriate lawyers and support staff required to increase the client's satisfaction with the firm. As team leader, the CRM should serve as a coach to team members. Some other duties of a CRM are to: identify the best team members to work on specific client projects; identify and strengthen team member skills; manage the client-focused team's relationship with outsiders and create opportunities for other members of the firm. The CRM should work with the team to develop pricing and alternative billing strategies for these key clients.

The CRM should work with the team members and firm management to develop relevant reward and recognition systems for the team members. What gets compensated gets done. The obvious benchmark of a successful CRM is when the client and the members of the firm's client-focused team meet and plan jointly for the upcoming year. This joint planning approach significantly reduces the adversarial tensions that can arise in relationships between inside and outside counsel.

Selecting Team Members for the Client-Focused Teams

First and foremost, the team members will need to be selected on the basis of the legal skills the client needs or will need. A willingness to be a team player is another asset. Experience has shown that the way we work as lawyers, "monks in a cloister," gives us little in the way of team experience. Our achievements, both academic and in practice, contribute to the "Lone Ranger Syndrome," a tendency to become self-contained and unwilling to seek outside advice. We are good, however, at working in teams on a specific billable project for the client. The CRM should select those team members who are willing to spend non-billable time in internal firm meetings focused on building more profitable client relationships. The team members will need to learn team building, as well as client development skills and must make time available to devote to client development. The CRM should select team members who are motivated to learn about the client's business and industry.

The Role of the Client-Focused Team Members

The major mission of team members is to execute the client-focused development plan that the team creates. The client-focused development plan should focus on increasing the client's satisfaction with the firm, increasing revenue and profitability and expanding or protecting the existing relationship. Clearly, a common firm-wide planning methodology must be agreed upon as the client-focused teams shift in size and composition depending on the needs of the client. Without a common planning methodology, team meetings deteriorate into "who do you know" discussions and the ability for lawyers to move effortlessly from team to team is difficult. The planning task appeals to most lawyers; planning is what lawyers like to do most. In the early stages of executing a plan, the team members need to collect information about the client's business strategies and *legal needs*. In addition, team members should help the team identify competitive threats. Many firms do not sense the competitive threat and very often do not track competitive activity.

A client-focused team member's knowledge of what, how much, how often and why your clients are buying from other service providers is critical to the team's strategy. This information should be gathered in face-to-face meetings with client decision makers and the information shared with the team members.* The face-to-face time with clients is the most useful element in execution of a plan, not the endless cycle of redrafting the internal written plan. If team members are reluctant to gather this information and to meet face-to-face periodically to share ideas and information, then the CRM needs to determine if they are meeting their team's *contract*.

"Who Else Is Doing This Client-Focused Teams Thing?"

Is this idea a radical notion or an old idea revisited? Who else is using this CRM and client-focused team approach? This approach is perhaps a throw-back to what partners and firms did in the first fifty years of this century to build both a firm's reputation and client relationships. The idea that a CRM is the firm's ambassador or account manager is not unique to industry or professional services organizations. Many large sales and service organizations--IBM, Xerox, airlines, financial institutions, accounting firms, advertising firms and a small number of law firms--have had account managers. The account manager, NAM (National Account Manager) or LAM (Large Account Manager) are currently being used with great success in accounting and consulting firms. Clients look upon these account managers as their resource. They assist clients in finding new and more profitable ways to manage their business. Most of the industry and accounting firms have formal training programs for these Large Account Managers.

Clients do not share the same feelings. Client acceptance of the accounting firm CRM has been so great that many businesses have allowed the accounting firm's CRM to office out of the client's location. The on-site accounting account manager is not a fad but rather a clear strategy to *seamlessly* integrate accounting services into the client's business strategies. There is strong cynical feeling among lawyers that these account managers are in place to exploit the client rather than help the client manage their accounting services needs. Do an informal survey of your key clients to determine which outside service providers have offices on their property. This a good indication of the trust that clients' have in accountants, consultants and outside vendors.

Most law firms are not currently organized in client or industry teams. Most are grouped by practice or by area of specialty. Exceptions are high-tech teams, health care, financial institutions, etc. Even these teams typically do not have all the lawyers that the client might need (real estate, employment, ERISA, trust and estates) on the team. The practice groups in firms have been functional work groups whose mission is to produce a work product, not manage the overall client-firm relationship. Without the benefit of client-focused teams, the client can drift from practice group to practice group like refugees seeking help from the firm's various independent "lawyer-states." Another impediment to creating teams is the knee jerk response when revenue goes down. Firm management responds by cutting internal firm operating costs and sending partners the "get your hours up" letter. As a firm's revenue picture becomes darker, the partners respond by client-hoarding and avoiding teams which has the effect of accelerating the downward revenue spiral and reducing opportunity.

Several firms varying in size from 12 lawyers to 700 lawyers are beginning to show signs of moving from soft marketing (brochures, newsletters, speeches and entertainment) to client-focused teams. One senior New York litigator characterized his firm's past efforts as "sissy marketing," a timid approach to marketing that fits partners' unwillingness to embark on anything other than traditional or soft marketing. It has been suggested by some managing partners that their firm's culture may not be consistent with the new team approach and the concept of selecting client managers may create internal firm competition for clients. Just the opposite should occur; cooperation and coordination is more likely to be the product of a well-managed team effort. Internal firm "food fights" over client control are occurring now in many firms without a clearly defined CRM or client-focused team approach. Several of these internal firm discussions have spilled over into the client's offices with disastrous effects. Who in the firm *owns* the client is the wrong discussion. The continued debate over what is right for the firm's culture is an internal focus that overlooks the external competitive threats and what is best for the client. Who can imagine a client that is not interested in a well-coordinated outside law firm's team which is clearly focused on their success in achieving their corporate and organizational objectives.

How To Get Started

Select a small group of clients where the client manager is an obvious non-threatening or political choice. Produce the spreadsheet report of practice areas and revenue, then call the first team meeting. To ensure success, have an agenda and a meeting start and stop time, a rarity in most firms today. Explain the mission of the CRM and the roles of the team to the meeting participants. Decide at this first meeting when to convene the planning session that will focus on the client. Give each team member background information on the client so the planning process will be effective. Create a computer database to collect and store information that comes from these internal and external client meetings. Report back to the firm's management the results of the first internal firm meeting and then get started on implementing the client-focused team approach. Experience has shown that an aggressive schedule involves 10 to 12 client-focused teams with a CRM and a plan in place within 12 months of inception. This team approach will be consistent with the client's view, a more competitive response in the marketing effort and create greater profitability for both the client and the firm.

*Author's note: The types of questions can be found in the *Texas Lawyer* (September 23, 1991) monograph entitled, "20 Questions You Should Ask Current and Prospective Clients."

A condensed version of this article appeared in the May 6, 2002 edition of *The National Law Journal* and the May 1995 issue of *The American Lawyer*.

FLANNERY & FLANNERY, L.L.P.
Annual Revenue History
in $000

Client	Real Estate	Corporate Securities	Employ. Law	Environ- mental	Litigation	T&E Planning	Tax	TOTAL	Opportunity $$	Market Share
Logic Solutions, Inc.	4	18	180		210		15	427		
ABC Manufacturing	75	17	35	22	87		99	335		
Strategic Systems	99	94			69		29	291		
ZEO Computers	10	13	35	44		45	66	213		
Lawn Games, Inc.					100			100		
First United Bank			2					2		
Total	188	142	252	66	466	45	209	1,368		

7

Attorney Training: A Consultant's Perspective

"...training and preparation can be the difference between winning and losing. The firm that trains its lawyers will have an edge - the competitive edge."

Many lawyers don't like to market because they feel that they lack the skills to market. They feel that they cannot be trained to do something that is a "natural born gift." Training lawyers to market can be difficult; however, every lawyer can learn to make rain.

One need not be an expert in marketing or client relations to realize that the vast majority of lawyers could benefit from formalized marketing and client development training. One of the stumbling blocks to training has been the lack of recognition by the lawyers that they need formalized training. Other major challenges are finding, developing or modifying available courses and instructors to meet the needs and the "culture" of the firm.

Your lawyers need an organized marketing training program if any of the following conditions exist in your firm:

- The lawyers don't make follow-up calls on prospective clients after the firm held a seminar, open house or other firm function.
- Less than 20 percent of the lawyers account for more than 80 percent of the new business origination.
- The lawyers spend more time in meetings talking about marketing than they spend in face-to-face marketing.
- The lawyers are not, nor have they been, asked to participate in competitive business presentations.
- The lawyers know little about their client's business outside of their immediate practice area.
- The lawyers cannot describe the firm in terms that clearly differentiates the firm from all other competitors.
- The lawyers say that they have a marketing program because the firm has retained a public relations consultant, hired a marketing director, or published a brochure or a newsletter.
- The lawyers describe marketing as concepts rather than real life activities, such as client presentations, calls on prospective clients or developing new clients.

Perhaps you have observed the frustration that your lawyers and the firm's managing partner feel when one or more of these conditions existed. The answer clearly lies with training. Firms that have taken on the training challenge report that their lawyers are taking the "next step." Their lawyers are proactive with clients and prospective clients. This new found confidence comes from a better understanding of how and why clients make decisions for legal services. The art of rainmaking has always been viewed with some degree of mystique. Many lawyers feel that personality type determines the rainmaker's success and, therefore, such skills cannot be taught. Despite this widely held belief, about 40 firms nationwide have decided to train their lawyers in marketing and client relationship management skills. The firms are in cities of all sizes. The firms vary in size from two to over 400 lawyers. Their clients, markets and practice areas vary widely. However, their strategy is the same...to be effective at marketing you must know how to do it in a systematic, ethical and professional way. These are skills that require formalized training.

An ideal training course should be designed to teach all of the firm's lawyers - partners, associates, rainmakers and "drought makers." The rationale is that all lawyers have clients, therefore, there is a need to learn client relationship skills. The single biggest impediment to implementing training has been lawyers who view marketing as either a passing fad or fear that it signals a firm in decline. These fears can also be the result of an attitude toward client development that sees all marketing activities as unethical or unproductive. These concerns must be aired and resolved early on if the training is to be successful.

The ideal course should not be a quick fix to a client or revenue crisis. Experience has shown that a two-day retreat is not adequate time to address concerns, train lawyers, implement a strategy and identify client opportunities. The size of the group to be trained should be small enough to allow for individual discussion; and ideal size is approximately 12 lawyers. The length of the training can vary but each lawyer should expect to spend at least 18 to 24 hours of combined class and workshop activities. The best way to train is to use a mock marketing case study. The case study should be as close to a real life client situation as possible, and should be designed so that it is sophisticated enough to challenge the lawyers to participate. You should also consider having several of your lawyers role play the general counsel or other executives in the hypothetical case study.

The next step is to videotape your lawyers making calls to these "clients." The tape clearly allows the lawyers to develop their listening and questioning skills. Because much of marketing is face-to-face meetings, the videotaping allows the lawyers to view their nonverbal communications skills, or body language. The instructor should spend time with lawyers individually to help them develop their strengths and work on their weaknesses. An added benefit is that often new hidden marketing talent is discovered and encouraged. Another tool for effective learning is to divide the group of 12 lawyers in half and have them compete for the business with this hypothetical client. Lastly, the training should include how to compete in the business presentation environment...the beauty contests.

Most firms have not considered training their lawyers. Instead they have spent both time and energy on brochures, seminars, newsletters, articles, speeches and client entertainment. These activities still play a role in developing business. The real test for marketing effectiveness is if your lawyers are able to use these support materials in their calls on clients and develop more profitable business relationships.

Several firms have institutionalized their training. The first-year associates are given an introductory course and each class after that receives additional training each year. This enables the firm to have a well-trained group of partners later on without having to ask the partners to give up substantial time. Several firms have been successful in obtaining CLE credit for the training.

Currently, marketing training is a hot subject within the ranks of lawyers, legal administrators and marketing directors. The questions for your lawyers are:

- Can I make an effective marketing call?
- Can I make calls without training?
- Am I willing to learn new skills?
- Will I devote the time to be trained?
- What are the alternatives - mentoring, watching a video course, reading an article?
- Who will do the training?

Many lawyers are skeptical of marketing training and don't want to be on the "leading edge." Therefore, the most frequently asked question is "Who else is doing this?" As in any competitive situation, training and preparation can be the difference between winning and losing. The firm that trains its lawyers will have an edge - the competitive edge.

ATTORNEY TRAINING

This article appeared in the Fall 1990 issue of the *Marketing Management Newsletter*.

Opinion Surveys Can Help Firms Keep Clients Happy

"The client opinion survey is one of the best ways to measure client satisfaction."

For a law firm to survive, it must serve its clients well. Yet most firms do not have an organized method to evaluate their clients' perceptions of the firm's performance. Without client feedback, the firm's management cannot determine the strength of the relationship.

The client opinion survey is one of the best ways to measure client satisfaction. A well-designed and properly conducted survey also can provide information that will help the firm make decisions on marketing, growth, fee determination and practice emphasis.

Questions to be considered by a firm planning to conduct a client opinion survey include:

• What is the survey's purpose?

The purpose will dictate the type of information to be collected. Most firms will find themselves in an endless debate trying to determine what each lawyer wants to see on the survey. A way to avoid that trap is to designate a small group of lawyers and the appropriate support staff to define the purpose and select the survey questions.

• Who should be surveyed?

Business and institutional clients are accustomed to participating in customer-satisfaction surveys and probably would participate in written or face-to-face programs on an annual basis. The most important clients of the firm should be interviewed face-to-face in the client's office.

Certain types of consumer practices, personal injury, bankruptcy, and family law need to get feedback from clients immediately. These clients should be surveyed using comment cards after every office visit.

• Who should conduct the survey?

This is another topic that can cause endless debate. The firm should delegate the management of the program to no more than three or four lawyers and the firm's marketing director. Although many lawyers believe that the best people to conduct the survey are public relations agencies and consultants, an effective survey is one that gets to the bottom of the issues, and outsiders don't always know the proper follow-up questions to ask. Surveys also can be opportunities to market the firm's capabilities, and outsiders obviously cannot perform that function.

The most critical qualifications for the people conducting the survey are the abilities to communicate and to show empathy, trust and concern for the client's well-being. The interviewers also should have some knowledge of the client's business and key decision makers and should have received training in listening skills and questioning techniques.

Most of the initial interviews will be face-to-face, and training in body language or semiotics (non-verbal communications) will be important. The training should include a pretest of the questionnaire, with the interviewers being videotaped conducting interviews with mock clients.

• When should the survey be conducted?

Now. Client satisfaction is the best measure of a firm's stability and future. Firms that don't have a way to measure

FLANNERY ON BUSINESS DEVELOPMENT, MARKETING,
AND SALES FOR LAWYERS

client satisfaction will eventually see the results of poor client relationships in less-palatable ways than merely unpleasant answers to a survey.

The most obvious is when the client fires the firm. Often a client feels hurt because of the firm's perceived indifference and shifts its business away from the firm quietly and without the firm's knowledge.

This scenario often is accompanied by a panic attack by the firm or a "diplomatic mission" to determine why the firm no longer is getting its share of the client's legal business. If the firm has to ask for its "fair share," it probably is too late to save the relationship.

Although many firms are reluctant even to broach the subject of client surveys for fear of offending their partners, this reluctance needs to be overcome. Some partners may feel they are being pressured or scrutinized unfairly. The firm needs to help them realize that this is not the purpose of the survey. The firm also needs to recognize and accept that it may hear bad news from its clients.

Clients are not reluctant to give their opinions, and firms that ask the tough questions generally are viewed as caring and attentive. It is clear that the best way to determine client satisfaction is to ask the client.

Interview Blueprint

The interviewing techniques will be critical to the success of the relationship between the firm and the client and the quality of the information the firm receives. The questions should be open and allow for detailed feedback. The questioning style should avoid interrogating the client.

If the client should become offended or confrontational, the interviewer should employ reflective listening techniques to understand the true nature of the client's dissatisfaction.

The following are areas that should be discussed and tailored for each client interview:

1.   An evaluation of the firm's performance on all matters.

2.   Performance evaluation of the specific practice areas used by the client.

3.   Performance evaluation of the partner responsible for the client.

4.   Performance evaluation of the other lawyers who have worked on the client's matters.

5.   Performance evaluation of the quality of service provided in document preparation, informational systems support, paraprofessional support, telephone and voice mail, electronic mail and facsimile communications, and administrative support.

6.   Quality of advice and counsel.

7.   Quality of the work product.

8.   Firm's recognition and fulfillment of client's needs.

9.   Clarity of the billing procedures and fee arrangements.

10. Accessibility of the firm's partners and other key personnel.

11. Whether the firm has kept the client informed.

12. The firm's strengths and weaknesses.

13. The firm's reputation within the community or industry.

14. Areas for improvement.

15. Competitive analysis - the firm compared to other firms or alternatives.

16. Willingness to refer others to the firm.

17. Value the client has received for its investment in the firm.

18. The client's view of the firm's approach to matters on which it has worked.

19. Responsiveness of the individual lawyers and the firm to the client.

20. How the firm has shown that it cares about the client.

Implementing A Survey

The basic steps from the time the firm decides that a client survey makes good sense until the completion of the survey are:

- Select a management team.
- Select clients to be surveyed.
- Create the questions for the survey.
- Select the interviewers.
- Train the interviewers.
- Conduct the survey.
- Review the results and take action.

The missing link in these steps is what to do after you learn that you have a client dissatisfaction problem. That next step is to implement a client relationship management program. A more common name is client development. Some firms call client-satisfaction programs by another name - marketing. The real challenge for most firms is to get started doing something other than talking about client satisfaction.

Clients often comment that lawyers need to pay more attention to the client's bottom line rather than their own. Client opinion surveys are unique tools for assessing the quality of the relationship with a client and at the same time determine how the client feels about the firm's contribution to the client's bottom line.

Without a client opinion survey, there is no ongoing, positive way for a firm to measure the success of its service strategy and its clients' perception of that strategy.

This article appeared in the June 11, 1990 issue of *Texas Lawyer*.

9

A Survival Plan for the '90s:
The New Age of Marketing

Lawyers Must Learn Direct Sales Skills

"But lawyers looking for the most productive way of re-maining competitive and producing new business in the 1990s will have to go one step further - direct marketing calls."

Most law firms are familiar with the traditional and most popular forms of marketing their services to the business community. But the old standbys - speeches, written articles, seminars, newsletters, brochures, community service, media and public relations - will not be as affective in the future. These forms of marketing will continue to be necessary to maintain a firm's visibility in the community. But lawyers looking for the most productive way of remaining competitive and producing new business in the 1990s will have to go one step further - direct marketing calls.

The two primary reasons causing the change are:
• Clients and prospective clients are forcing lawyers and firms to use more direct methods of marketing.

- Increased competition from other firms is creating a need for firms to differentiate themselves.

Recently, decision makers for legal services have been asking law firms to make formal presentations, commonly referred to as "beauty contests," and to respond to bids for services using a request for proposal (RFP).

This approach gives the decision makers a way to differentiate among the competing firms. There is also a sense of fairness in the selection process and the organization generally benefits by getting the best deals, lowest cost or both.

Direct marketing calls on the decision makers are the best way for firms to gather information to respond to the RFP and the beauty contests. Direct marketing calls also can be used to communicate the firm's uniqueness and determine the selection criteria.

Comparative Shopping

Recently a large hospital engaged in comparative "shopping," asking outside law firms to respond to an RFP and make a formal presentation. Six firms responded with extensive presentations and brochures designed specifically for the hospital.

The successful firm formed a special marketing team to respond to the client's requests. The team was made up of lawyers in the health care practice as well as lawyers from other practice areas. Members of the team made direct calls on the decision makers prior to the presentation to determine the needs and the selection criteria. The lawyers developed a tailored response to the RFP and they rehearsed the presentation several times.

In short, they prepared for this encounter as if it were an important trial.

Making direct calls and rehearsing the presentation was a unique response for the firm and probably increased the firm's odds of winning the business.

Other examples of the same comparative techniques are: a state university system requested "bids" and presentations for

ERISA work; an entertainment complex used the beauty contest to select outside counsel; a large Texas-based airline and an out-of-state retailer used both the presentation and the RFP.

Some firms have gone on the offensive and developed unique marketing programs to head off the RFP and beauty contests. A 23-lawyer firm, anticipating the beauty contest and RFP, made marketing calls on a bank's decision makers. After learning the client's specific needs, the firm created a presentation on lender liability. Although the firm's presentation was offered as an educational seminar for the bank, it allowed the firm to showcase its knowledge and experience in a way that made it stand out from the pack.

The firm practiced the presentation, used overhead transparencies and created a special workbook on lender liability. The firm was successful in retaining the client and, in fact, its business increased, requiring the addition of several new lawyers.

These presentations and marketing efforts take time, but the opportunity is significant. It has been estimated that there is approximately $100 million in outside legal fees that Dallas-area businesses have sent to firms outside the state. It is probably fair to assume that these decision makers are using the same or similar comparative techniques to select lawyers.

Clients Make The Rules

Although many lawyers and firms are reluctant to compete, it is the clients that are the decision makers and they set the rules for competition. Frequently, lawyers will admit privately that they don't like this new environment and are not confident that they have the marketing skills to compete.

There has been a great deal of frustration and discomfort associated with crossing the threshold from the familiar and traditional client lunch into the arena of competitive and direct marketing.

Direct marketing or "sales" skills were not taught in law school, or for that matter, until recently, anywhere else.

The art of rainmaking, bringing in clients and business, has always been viewed with some degree of mystique. Many lawyers feel that it is a personality type that determines the rainmaker's success and, therefore, these skills cannot be taught. Despite this widely held belief, about 15 firms nationally (five in Texas), have decided to view marketing and selling skills training differently.

The firms vary widely in size, practice areas and clients, but their strategy is the same. They are training all of their lawyers - partners, associates, rainmakers and mist makers - in direct selling and communication skills. They reason that because all lawyers have clients, then all lawyers need to maintain those client relationships and develop business.

The trick is to turn the mist makers into more than mist makers and the rainmakers into monsoon makers.

Training lawyers to use these skills can include role playing using case studies of client marketing opportunities. Lawyers make marketing call with a "client," an exercise that helps develop questioning and listening skills and allows lawyers to experience marketing problems firsthand.

Because much of direct marketing is nonverbal communications, or body language, videotaping the marketing calls can improve the lawyer's nonverbal communications. Videotaping also can be used to improve the lawyer's business presentation skills.

The Team Approach

Lawyers trained in direct marketing can form a marketing team that meets periodically to develop a tailored marketing program for a specific client or prospective client.

The typical team might be composed of lawyers from four or five different practice groups. A typical strategy might be to enhance the current relationship with the client and increase revenue for the firm. The ultimate objective of the training and targeting is to understand the client's needs and market relevant solutions that head off the RFP and the beauty contest.

Most firms have overlooked training and instead have spent their resources in the indirect marketing area, such as brochures, seminars, newsletters, etc. The new wave of brochures that are out on the streets are second and third generation.

Seminars on various business and legal issues are given by law firms weekly in various metropolitan cities in Texas. Newsletters, unheard of 10 years ago, are selling specialized practice groups in high tech, banking, labor, tax, etc.

All these efforts are needed, but the majority of this material could be analogized to a travel agent's tour and destination information package. The maps, hotel lists, restaurants and sightseeing brochures are part of the trip preparation. However, the travelers (lawyers) need to know that basics of driving the car (direct marketing). It is clear that, until the basics have been covered, the journey cannot begin.

Once under way, some will want to drive faster than others, some will not want to drive at all. But to make the journey successful, every lawyer will have to spend some time in the driver's seat, i.e., direct marketing.

Some lawyers will make mistakes: missing signals, not recognizing or heeding signs, and moving too fast for some clients. Many will try to avoid the experience altogether by relying on the old ways - promotional materials, public relations firms or marketing directors to do their marketing.

But direct marketing is the domain of lawyers, and a firm will need to involve every lawyer in its marketing efforts to survive in the 1990s.

Pack Mentality

One of the more frequently asked questions from lawyers is, "Who else is doing this?" Many lawyers and firms will wait too long to answer that question. Other firms will recognize the need for direct marketing and take action in time to beat their competition and keep valued clients.

Any article on marketing would not be complete without a word on ethics. Initially, the most successful and rewarding efforts in marketing will come from marketing to current clients. Clearly, marketing to existing clients is ethical and cross-selling additional services of the firm to these clients will be the easiest first step.

It also is ethical to market in situations where the firm has been asked to bid or participate in a beauty contest by a prospective client.

Generally it costs five times as much to market to prospective clients as it does to existing clients. Therefore, as an economic consideration, firms should spend their time and resources marketing to their existing clients and avoid the ethical mine fields associated with "cold calls" and prospecting. The experience gained from "client-only marketing" can eventually be used in attracting prospective clients.

This article appeared in the November 6, 1989 issue of *Texas Lawyer*.

10

10 Reasons Why Law Firm Marketing Is Failing and How To Fix The Problems

In a buyer's market not responding to the buyer's needs is a benchmark of failure. Many lawyers and law firm marketing strategies are products looking for a market and disregard the client's needs. Symptoms of these strategies is an emphasis on selling without focus, a general lack of market research and pricing actions (lowering fees) designed to garner market share without regard to profitability. Differentiation and a focus on service are the strategies that will prove to be successful in the next 24 - 36 months. To implement any successful strategy, the firm will need to remove the impediments to implementation. These are the major impediments to the firm's success:

1)   **Compensation** - Compensation should be designed to encourage profitable behavior. A focus on individual rewards for business generation creates an atmosphere of client hoarding and an "eat what you kill" behavior. Client origination credits are equally counter productive. Often partners inherit clients and are unjustly rewarded when they had little or nothing to do with the continued success and profitability of the relationship. Firms will need to create client-focused relationship teams and reward the members of the team proportionally to their contributions.

This will mean that certain team members will be paid to manage the relationship and others for doing the work. Firms should reward individual attorneys when they assist in finding opportunities in practice areas other than their own. In marketing, the rule is: What gets compensated gets done.

2)   **Focus** - Most firms and individuals spend time and resources trying to create demand and generate leads. This behavior is generally linked to a compensation system which rewards new client matters and does not pay for additional business from current clients. Law firm leaders should calculate where 85% of the firm's business comes from and select key individuals to manage those client relationships. The objective should be to focus on business preservation. Another important activity is to grow and expand relationships with current clients that use only a few services of the firm.

3)   **Skills** - There is a widely held belief in law firms that it takes a certain personality to be a successful rain maker. Effective legal services marketing are skills that can be learned. New successful approaches to teaching interpersonal communications skills and marketing as a business process have been developed over the last fifteen years that can turn drought makers into rain makers. The stereotype "rain maker": out going, gregarious and "close the business" type is no longer the model that is working. This is especially true in a buyer's market. There are methodical and systematic business processes for determining buyers' needs. These approaches are far more successful with sophisticated clients. Most firms don't understand the need to train their lawyers in these new business process and communications skills. Subscribe to business and marketing journals as a way of providing new information and insights.

4)   **Leadership** - Leaders can be defined by those who achieve objectives through the efforts of others. To be a successful leader one must have a clear vision of the direction the

firm needs to be going. Leaders must be able to communicate this vision to everyone. Leaders will need to be clear about how they plan to implement the vision and be responsible for the success or failure of that vision. Too often managing partners micro-manage and lose the "big picture". Leaders need to be focused on creating a firm culture and leave the day-to-day management of business to administrators.

5)   **Hourly Billing** - "We have no time to market, we have to bill hours." Clients are forcing change in the way lawyers bill. Hourly billing as a way of doing business is creating problems for the buyers of legal services. They cannot budget for matters effectively. They cannot manage the process without adding costs and lastly there is no incentive for the law firm to improve efficiency. When project billing becomes the norm lawyers will have more time to market and develop clients. In the mean time, the firm should develop a set of guidelines to help the partners and associates determine if it makes sense to spend time doing billable work for unprofitable clients verses the alternative which is to spend non-billable time focused on marketing to profitable clients.

6)   **Marketing Plans** - Individual marketing plans are good except where everyone in the firm wants to do work for the firm's largest client and the efforts are not coordinated. Many consultants have discovered that lawyers like to spend time planning rather than doing. As a result, consultants have wasted firm resources developing individual, practice group and firm marketing plans. Their efforts are generally focused on the planning and drafting of a carefully crafted plan. Having completed the plan, there is little money, time and energy left for the execution. The plan generally begins to gather dust. A simple plan to focus on those clients who are responsible for 85% of the firm's revenue will be more successful.

7)   **Denial** - "The business will continue to come to the firm no matter what." "Someone else will market for me." "I bring in $3 million now, what or why do I need to improve?" This is death wish marketing. Complacency about your firm's need to continuously improve service and the firm's marketing efforts is a prescription for lower profitability. All firms have partners who are in denial. The trick is to make a change in the way the firm's lawyers work with clients and encourage those efforts that are consistent with the firm's culture and values.

8)   **Infrastructure** - Most firms have devoted too little re-source to marketing. Many firms don't use the resources they have profitably. The firm will need to spend time and money to produce high quality proposals and presentations. Staff will need to be trained in the basics of client focused service. If the firm is large enough (15 lawyers) then a marketing or client rela-tions director may be needed. The best way to determine the need is to measure the time the lawyers spend in non-lawyer ac-tivities devoted to client development.

9)   **Teamwork** - Why aren't there more teams in law firms? Ego and lack of team experience coupled with the rugged indi-vidualism fueled by the competitive educational system inhibits the creation and implementation of teams. It's not a coincidence that law firms have practice groups, not teams. Client-focused teams offer the client more value and the firm the opportunity to manage the relationship profitability. Our success as lawyers has been the result of individual effort. We are reluctant to rely on other team members for success. Try team training and team exercises using real life experiences.

10)   **Technology** - Law firm software and computer systems were not designed to provide profitability, market trends, and related client databases. Most firms use their technology as big calculators and expensive typewriters. Develop a client-focused database. You should be able to ask the system to provide: who

are our most profitable clients, what do they buy, how often, who buys (G.G., business people, etc.), and are they satisfied? The best way to get the technology working for the firm is to write out the marketing reports you would like to receive and work backwards to the creation of the database. Buy desk top publishing software and create a presentation and proposal center.

These are the major impediments and they will require attention and action. Too many lawyers get caught up in the elegance of the planning process, fail to take action and eventually go into marketing denial and paralysis. The answers lie with action. We are, as a profession, reluctant to try new ideas or approaches. The reluctance is partially due to fear of failure but it is also a desire to find the perfect solution. Most of the important business discoveries were the result of mistakes while trying to find a solution to a known problem.

The best way to remove these impediments is to recognize and communicate the problems firm-wide. The debate that it will occur will be generally focused on the means, process, etc. rather than the end result. Keep asking your partners the same questions: If we don't change, what will be the consequences over the next several months? If a loss of profit, clients or partners is the result, then start working on making a change to remove the impediments to successful client development. Each individual lawyer in the firm will have to make a change and there lies the challenge. John Kenneth Gailbraith said it best: "Faced with the choice between changing one's mind and proving there is no need to do so almost everyone gets busy on the proof." As lawyers, we have been spending too much on proof and not enough on action.

This article appeared in the February 1995 issue of the *Texas Bar Journal* as an excerpt to an article by Melinda Smith.

11

Importance of Training

One or two rainmakers cannot carry your law firm through the '90s. We need more lawyers out there who know how to get the most out of their marketing role. The answer lies in training.

The need for lawyer training hinges on how many firm rainmakers you want. Rainmakers are generally self-taught and their methods, although effective, may not be the one that novice marketers should learn and adopt. Professionals, however, can train lawyers to make marketing easier for them, to reduce the time commitment and to "fix their game."

Marketing is not a natural skill, but lawyers can develop it and the results are trained lawyers who consistently develop clients more effectively and profitably.

What benefits can your firm expect to derive from having your lawyers trained? Training:

- Builds better communications skills.
- Develops hidden talent.
- Ensures consistent quality.
- Provides greater focus.
- Produces more effective/productive efforts.
- Clarifies the concept of marketing as a business process.

In the beginning, a firm should use professionals to train - at least the first time. Choosing the right professional can be difficult and requires systematic review:
- Evaluate their experience.
- Sit in on a training session.
- Verify that they can withstand attack.
- See if they can look beyond the quick fix.
- Confirm that they provide an interactive program.
- Check references as to what training survived and how it has been used.

It's best not to use academics or professors who may not be practical in their approach; product sales instructors who know an entirely different process from the one that successfully markets services; accountants who *The Wall Street Journal* says know little about clients and less about the firm; and videos or tapes, which are only good support materials.

The best training programs are off-site in an atmosphere conducive to learning. The date should be scheduled well in advance, allowing time during the session for breaks. The best results are achieved in small group workshops and discussions using a hands-on style, as well as case studies and visuals.

JoAnn Martindale, marketing director for Dallas' Gardere & Wynne, suggests that the lack of understanding and time constraints are obstacles to a training program. Lawyers often "fear" the process, anticipating rejection or embarrassment or identification of their behavior as offensive. They may fail to see the many benefits of the training.

Training builds teams by expanding a lawyer's knowledge of the firm, by teaching him or her to trust the skills of others, and by increasing the credibility of the in-house marketing professional. It also elevates awareness and the status of marketing, and creates tangible results as well as a monitoring system.

The best of all training worlds is the one-on-one approach, which combines skill building with encouragement of the conceptual thinking needed for successful marketing. The program should include a clear definition of marketing. Development of good communications skills and business psychology should be part of the program. Lawyers will be taught to conduct clients meetings, make telephone calls, evaluate results, seize opportunities, and understand buyer psychology and motivation. Information gathering and use of supporting materials round out successful training programs.

Any training program must include practical applications, follow-up techniques that make the effort a habit, and both tangible and intangible rewards. The real clue to successful training is the follow-through, which employs activity recaps, client reviews, plan revisions and assignments complete with deadlines.

After successful training, lawyers exhibit new skills, see new opportunities, have greater confidence and a sense of direction, contribute to the firm and are motivated to action. Training allows every lawyer to play a more significant role in the marketing process. Lawyers become an organized, focused and strategic force to be reckoned with.

This article appeared in the May 1990 issue of *Marketing for Lawyers*.

12

How To Teach Your Lawyers To "Sell"
or
Can We Turn Drought Makers Into Rainmakers?

The format of this article is a letter to the managing partner out-
lining the why and what the firm should do in marketing,
business development or client development.

Memo to: Managing Partner

From: Director of Client Relations/Law Firm
            Administrator/Executive Director

Subject: Teaching our lawyers to "sell"

If we are to be more successful at developing business
and increasing profitability, we will need to help our lawyers to
learn new skills, modify their individual behavior and change
their attitude about marketing and selling legal services. We
may have to, at a later date, look at changing the firm's reward
and recognition (compensation systems) to encourage the appropriate new behavior. It is clear to me that we need to quit talking

about business development and begin taking action. Training is the first step.

If clients and prospective clients buy legal services from lawyers directly and not from seminars, brochures, newsletters, etc. then our lawyers should be expected to develop the lion's share of the business by meeting clients face-to-face. Clearly opportunities for business will continue to come from our seminars, newsletters, brochures, speeches, client outings and the articles we have written. However, we will need to be more effective at taking these opportunities and developing them into clients or expanding current client relationships. Therefore, the emphasis should be on teaching our lawyers to be more effective at those face-to-face client and prospective client meetings. The skills we will need to teach our lawyers are simple. The bigger challenge will be to modify their behavior and change their attitudes. We will not be able to force change or use fear as the method of motivation. Perhaps we should consider a change in the course emphasis and a title that focuses on current client relationships. The tone and title of the course will go a long way to making business development more acceptable. We could call the course "Building and Maintaining Effective Client Relationships." We may want to delete the words marketing and selling from the firm's lexicon.

We should select a group of no more than three lawyers to be our curriculum development committee. This would allow the lawyers to put their fingerprints on the course and increase firm-wide acceptance. We will need to be sensitive to the NIH (Not Invented Here) syndrome. We may want to suggest to the curriculum development committee that they consider having an announced course goal. An example might be: To teach lawyers how to establish and develop more profitable relationships with existing and new clients.

The key subjects we may want to teach:
- Listening and personal communications skills
- Understanding client's communications styles and decision making

• Conducting face-to-face client and prospective client legal services needs interviews

• Understanding how clients choose their outside lawyers and law firms

• Client retention strategies and developing clients relationships effectively

• Increasing client satisfaction and quality service management strategies

• Developing client legal service planning and creating firm-wide client service teams

• Developing a client based Total Quality Management (TQM) strategy

The course probably should use communications skills tests, short lectures, structured group discussions, workshops, team exercises and real client case studies as the teaching methods. As part of the case studies we could either use clients or "outsiders" to role-play mock clients. We could have our lawyers "visit" these mock clients. The purpose would be to practice using the skills they would be learning in the course. It might be interesting if we video-taped the mock client visits and played the tapes back as a self-diagnostic learning tool. Video-taping will not be new, most CLE courses in trial skills, presentations skills, client interviewing and client counseling use the video-taping approach to learning. The other alternative is to buy pre-recorded sales training courses. There are several good video-taped "selling" programs that we could buy. We could use these taped courses as supplemental material. If we showed the tapes we would need to caution our lawyers that these canned programs may not represent the circumstances they will encounter. We could also use the tapes as a way of either developing our own taped series or as a catalyst for group discussion.

PARTICIPANTS: We will have to train all partners and associates. We will need to give everyone the opportunity to learn

93

these important skills. To get the firm's attention, the initial group should be the firm's leadership. Leadership by example will go a long way to changing everyone's view of the importance of the need to focus on increasing business. We should start with a small control group of no more than eight to ten. Afterward we can make a judgment about increasing the size of the group.

LENGTH and LOCATION of the COURSE: Two to three consecutive days and several follow-up sessions. Anything shorter would be viewed as cursory, not substantive and probably wouldn't cause the desired change in behavior. We will need to consider doing this training off-site to avoid constant interruptions.

INSTRUCTORS: It is my view that the success of the course will be mostly related to the instructor's abilities. The instructor(s) should have a high energy level, good communications skills and an ability to gain the respect of the participants. One absolute rule is: The instructor must not be boring. There should be some passion and enthusiasm about the subject matter. In selecting the right person we have several options. All them have their pros and cons. I thought I might compare several potential training instructors and their approaches.

Professional Trainers

Pro: They have the teaching and course development skills.

Con: Expense and familiarity with lawyers and the firm's culture may be a limitation.

Law Firm Consultants

Pro: Experience and knowledge about lawyers and firms.

Con: Lack of teaching and course development skills. They may want to cross sell the firm unneeded consulting services.

Our Firm's Rainmakers

Pro: They understand the firm and are successful at "selling".

Con: The rainmaker's style may not be appropriate for everyone and could cause resentment and negative vibes. Often, they themselves do not know nor can they teach the secrets of their success. Teaching rainmaking by mentoring is largely a myth.

Marketing Professors

Pro: They have written books and teach marketing in business schools. They understand the concepts.

Con: These people are usually good at concepts and theory but frequently they lack practical experience. It is often said that they are teaching because they can't make a living themselves doing what they teach others to do.

Marketing Professionals

Pro: They know business and marketing at the practical day-to-day level. They may have been clients and may understand the buyers' motivations and needs.

Con: They can sell products and services but may not be able to teach lawyers or law firms the skills to develop clients and business.

Law Firm Support Staff

Pro: Law firm administrators and marketing directors know the lawyers and the firm. They may have an understanding of what needs to be taught.

Con: You can never be a prophet in your own house. They may need to deliver bad news to the unsuccessful trainees and thus creating unneeded enemies. They may not have teaching experience.

Clients Instructors

Pro: Great idea that can be a client relationship builder.

Con: More preaching than teaching. The lawyers may discount the message and shoot the messenger. Clients may lack the skills to teach. Clients may be shocked at their lawyer's lack of knowledge and skills. The clients could become openly critical during the training.

I recommend we select the curriculum development committee ASAP. Their role will be to develop the course, select the instructor(s) and implement the course. As I suggested, we may want to announce to the firm our intentions. We should be careful to avoid the message that the training is a remedial rainmaking course or that the firm is in desperate need of business. We will need to have several follow-up sessions after the initial training as a way to identify our successes and necessary course corrections. The follow-up sessions will help us make adjustments in the course to insure a reality-based training program. The follow-up sessions could also serve as a way to identify the business that came as a direct result of the training.

We should expect to spend between $1000 to $3000 per lawyer to train. As a comparison, off-the-shelf generic corporate marketing or sales training programs that are worth their salt are priced at $1500 to $3000 per student. It would only take an increase in fees of approximately $5,000 per lawyer over the course of their career to give the firm a payback for the lawyer's time and training cost. The other benefit to the training will be that we will enhance the quality of our relationships with our current clients and reduce client defections. In these recessionary times, client retention is important. It costs five times as much to find a new client as it takes to keep our current profitable clients. Therefore, we should train to retain! Lastly, we may not have an opportunity later to train our lawyers when the economy turns around and they become too busy or complacent to invest their time in training.

This article appeared in the *ALA Marketing Management* newsletter in the Spring of 1992.

13

Technology and Marketing:
The Profitable Marriage

"Most firms have not figured out how to use technology to market their services."

What would you do if you were offered an extra hour, every day of the year, to use as you please? That would be an extra $73,000 more a year in billable work for those who bill at $200 an hour; or two full weeks of additional vacation or of time for a neglected hobby or interest; or 90 four-hour client development dinners or seminar presentations.

Suppose further that not only would these benefits cost you nothing in lost opportunity, but that you would be operating more effectively in those hours in which you did work?

If you were a lawyer, you would flee from this offer as you would from the plague.

How do we know this? Because this offer has been on the table for a number of years, and very few attorneys have seized it. We're referring to the fact that technology has unquestionably reached a point beyond the initial hype where it truly enables you to fit more into the 24-hour day.

Law firms have seized this opportunity in certain areas, such as billing and timekeeping; but in their marketing programs they're still playing with an abacus. As competition continues to tighten and marketing requires even greater effort, this problem will grow exponentially. While law firms search for ways to recoup technology costs, they resolutely ignore a substantial opportunity at their feet. The ultimate goal of marketing is to increase the firm's bottom line. Part of the marketing process is the exchange of information between the law firm and the buyer. Traditional marketing activities include: brochures and newsletters; open house receptions; visiting clients; and presentations for business. Marketing is also responding to RFPs (Requests For Proposals), communicating with clients using technology, tracking the firm's marketing efforts and analyzing the financial results of the firm's marketing efforts. The sad fact is very few firms are using technology to communicate with clients, make presentations or track the effectiveness of their marketing efforts. The business case for using technology to market legal services is a significant return-on-investment.

A few leading-edge firms are using personal computers to create databases to use for RFPs. These firms also create slides, overheads and multimedia, business development presentations using specialized presentation software. They are using the Internet and powerful laptop computers equipped with overhead projection displays (LCDs) to make business development presentations. Such users are also using technology to effectively manage client relations.

Managing Client Relationships

E-Mail can be an effective tool to transmit the firm's marketing message as well as handle routine communications with the firm's clients. Many of the larger firms have given selected clients access to the firm's E-Mail system to speed up the flow of communication, to foster contact and to utilize electronic billing. Communications with clients can also be made through organizations such as CompuServe, Lexis Counsel Connect and America On Line. On-line services are also a good source of business information on prospective and existing clients. Where communications are confidential, documents can be encrypted to insure that they are not read by the wrong party.

Project management software can be used to schedule complicated tasks such as initial public offerings, commercial loan transactions and litigation. Such software allows the user to readily make modifications to reflect changed conditions in the project such as schedules and responsibilities. Project management software coupled with electronic spreadsheets allow the lawyer to run sophisticated "what if" scenarios to help the client pick the optimal course of action. This is especially useful in evaluating litigation strategies and the economics of the matter.

Project management software coupled with client contact software can be used by the firm to track the firm's marketing efforts and results. To be effective, the firm must know what efforts are bearing fruit and devise appropriate rewards for the attorneys whose efforts are successful. Failure to reward successful marketing efforts will guarantee a marketing campaign which will be dead on arrival.

Document assembly software, which allows the practitioner to quickly assemble a single document to a group of related documents, constitutes another way the computer literate practitioner can maximize the return on technology. With clients increasingly demanding more innovative billing arrangements and more productivity from their service providers, document assembly software properly used can make the practitioner more competitive on smaller matters.

A Case Study

To understand how to apply technology, a quick case study can put things into perspective. Assume that an important client calls and asks that the firm be prepared to give a proposal and oral presentation the next day in a new practice area. Can you respond quickly? How can technology help?

The steps for creating any marketing proposal and presentation are:

- Planning and Research,
- Create Proposal,
- Create Presentation,
- Rehearse, and
- Present Capabilities.

Planning and Research

On-line information services are readily available and can be accessed to provide up-to-date business information on the client. Information such as recent public filings, press releases, and industry analyses are all available on-line from a variety of service providers. Legal services such as Lexis/Nexis can also be a provider of business data as well as more specific up-to-date information on any legal issues which need to be addressed. An additional source of information is Lexis Counsel Connect ("LCC"). This service provides a forum where counsel can communicate in an informal matter on issues, locate other attorneys who have specific expertise and provide a central location for team members to communicate electronically. For instance, LCC allows users to set up secure electronic conference and mail centers in which users can share documents and information.

Software products such as Lotus Notes are now available which allow the practitioner to share documents and spreadsheets across various types of computers. If the information is available, it is likely that it is accessible electronically and can be incorporated into the user's work product. All members of the client team should be tied together by E-Mail to insure prompt communication of information. *The ultimate goal of this process is to know as much about the client's business as the client does before making the presentation and to insure that this information is shared in a timely manner with the entire team.*

Create Proposal

Once the team has been identified and the relevant information gathered, the team can begin to assess what the outline of the client proposal should be. The Client Proposal should be tailored to meet the perceived needs and wants of the individual client. Having the attorney and staff biographies, previous firm experience, pricing and office logistical administration on-line will save production time. The proposal should be designed to show the client the level of the firm's interest in gaining the business and developing a relationship with the client. The proposal should include specific information on how, when and for what cost the firm can meet the client's needs. The proposal should also include information on how the firm will use the available technology to meet the needs of the client and add value to the relationship. Lotus Notes is useful when multiple locations of the firm are involved in creating the proposal. Clients are seeking a balance between fees, value and service. The presentation should clearly show how the firm is going to handle these issues.

Create Presentation

Once the details of the proposal are outlined, the firm can then look at how the information can best be communicated to the client in the form of an oral presentation. The presentation should include the following:
- A list of the firm's previous successes in dealing with the client's problems with companies which are close in size and structure to the client;
- Attorney and staff capabilities;
- The legal issues facing the client;
- A summary of how the firm will address the issues as well as a time line for doing so;
- The cost and fee structure to be used by the firm; and
- How the firm is going to use technology to give the client

up-to-date information and access to information so that the client can feel like it is part of the firm.

The key here is the differentiation and value which is added to the firm's services by integrating the client into the firm's information flow. For instance, in complex litigation and IPOs the firm could create a private database for the project which would include current drafts of documents, project time line information and cost data. Allowing the client access to such a database gives the client a feeling of being part of the team. It also gives the in-house attorney up-to-date information in areas which are important for internal reporting purposes. Clearly, for this concept to work the database and access rights needs to be tailored to the individual needs and desires of the client.

A successful 30 minute presentation will generally require ten (10) hours of preparation time. It should be rehearsed three (3) times by all participants in the group. It is helpful to have members of the firm who have not been involved in the preparation of the presentation come in to play the role of the company's officers. This is important because the presentation should not be a static talking head, one way flow of information. Rather, the successful presentation will create a dialog between the presenters and the client's representatives. Lawyers frequently worry about creating presentations which are too slick. However, the average business client is used to giving and receiving presentations which make full use of available high-tech multimedia capabilities. It makes sense then to use the methods of communication which the client is used to and not worry about being too slick. *The presentation should leave the client feeling that they have participated with the firm in arriving at workable solutions to the client's legal problems.*

Conclusion

Today's technology can not only provide the means in which the firm can produce work products, track expenses and prepare client bills, but it can also allow the firm to differentiate itself from the competition, provide tailored solutions to the client's legal needs, improve the flow of communication between the client and firm and increase the profitability by using technology in their marketing efforts.

This article is co-authored by Wayne J. Lovett and appeared in the September 11, 1995 edition of *Texas Lawyer*.

About The Author

Bill is the President of The WJF Institute, located in Austin, Texas. The Institute's primary focus is client development and client relationship management, law firm marketing and marketing support programs. The WJF Institute also trains lawyers and provides related consulting services in substantive legal skills, law firm management and leadership. Since 1988, The WJF Institute has conducted intensive, small group training sessions for over 14,000 attendees.

Bill graduated from the University of Maryland at College Park, MD in 1967. He started his career in 1966 at the Department of Justice as an instructor. He later joined the Johns-Manville Corporation in their Washington, DC office. In 1969, he joined the IBM Corporation in Washington, DC. While at IBM, he attended the University of Baltimore Law School and obtained his Juris Doctorate in 1973. He also attended the IBM/Harvard Advanced Business Executive Education Institute Program. His IBM career included assignments in marketing training, product marketing, large account marketing, corporate marketing planning, large system management, IBM corporate executive briefing program, corporate strategic planning, finance, litigation management, personal computer product development and technology for the legal profession. He was instrumental in creating a new IBM marketing group specializing in technology systems for the legal profession. The IBM Legal Profession Marketing Group was established in January 1980 in response to the growing technology systems needs of the private practice, courts, governments and in-house counsel here in the U.S. and overseas. As a member of IBM's Legal Profession Marketing Group, his responsibilities included IBM's relationships with key law firm computer customers, corporate law departments' in-house legal systems managers and IBM's outside counsel. He left IBM in 1988 and founded The WJF Institute.

Bill has been a special advisor to the ABA and the Association of Legal Administrators (ALA) on technology and marketing. He has served as a member of the ALA's Long Range Planning Committee. He was involved in developing and implementing the ALA's current long range plan. He has been a member of the ABA's Law School Curriculum Committee. He has lectured in law schools, graduate and undergraduate schools in the U.S. and overseas on strategic planning, technology and marketing. He has published numerous articles on marketing, technology and law firm management in law journals and legal publications. Bill is a frequent speaker at various legal conferences and meetings. The WJF Institute's Client Development and Relationship Management workshop was selected as a semi-finalist in Inc. magazine's Marketing Masters Awards in 1997 for innovative marketing programs.

Made in the USA
Charleston, SC
16 March 2012